WALK-ON ISLAND

Mastering the System to Get in the Game

TERRELL DOUGLAS

ISBN: 978-1-7359739-3-7
Library of Congress Control Number: 2021900143

For information contact :
Austin Brothers Publishers
http://www.abpbooks.com

First Edition: April 2021
Fort Worth, Texas

10 9 8 7 6 5 4 3 2 1

AUSTIN
BROTHERS PUBLISHING

I would like to dedicate this book to my beautiful mother Florence Marie Douglas. The understandings gained in adulthood open my eyes to the true gift that God allowed us with your presence. Your virtue and patience set a precident for how your three children are to approach the difficulties seen and unseen. Your hugs covered us, your words uplifted us and your kisses cemented the idea security within that pushed the three of us to be our best selves. The wisdom has and will always resonate throughout Dar'Ray, LaToya and my life. I love you and dedicate this to you.

Thank You/The Real MVPs

This piece was completed through growth and wisdom gifted by numerous individuals. Everyone will forever be reminded of how instrumental God and my mother Florence Douglas has been in my life. Everything you did was to build a better future for your children.

To my dad EC Douglas for showing the valuable lesson that its never too late to get better and to always be the best at whatever the task.

To my brother and sister who have always been my guardian angels. Thank you for the protection from the streets and you have always pushed me to stay on my grind big bro. Even when I got on your third last nerve you always had my back big sis

To my loves Jasmine and my baby cakes, I love you with all my heart and more.

To the rest of my Wilson/Lawson/Douglas/Yarborough families, who were always there to keep me balanced but also open minded always with examples of how to handle different types of situations.

To all of the coaches that have provided the knowledge for sports and life lessons.

To all who have been valued entities of this story Benjamin Adkins, Andre Bailey, Marcell Bates, Raynard Barnes, Wayne Beadle, Brannon Beasely, Sammy Brown, James Burden, Travis Bush, Everett Calloway, London Calloway, Phillip Causey, Bruce Cogdill, John Dansby III, Pastor Michael Evans Sr, Minister Carlos Francis, Gregory George, Adrian Harris, Lee Hayes, Michael Hayes, Justin Hicks, Minister Mikado Hinson, Crawford Jones, James Jones, Anthony Levine, Gregory Love, Ledarius Hicks, Chantal & David Mann Jr, Tamela & David Mann Sr, David Mason, Clarence McKinney, Joshua Peacock, Jordan Peppers, Victoria Schiebel, Mark Stout, Stephan Taylor, Kirk Thor, Jayven Tucker, and any others who I have missed

Y'all are the real MVPs

CONTENTS

Foreword

This book is written for the people or the athletes who have felt like they were constantly shit on. It's for those who had to play out of position for the good of the team, those who are still on the coach's shit list and were never given the opportunity. It's for the undervalued grinder who does their job daily, but someone else gets the credit. It's for those who didn't get the looks because their team wasn't overall successful enough, or because their school isn't in the right location.

It's for the misfit toys, the late bloomer, the undersized, the underappreciated, the too small, too short, too slow, not good enough arm, hands too small, arms not long enough, not talented enough, not smart enough, not quick enough, not fast enough, not strong enough, a little bit too crazy, a little bit too wild. Does any of that sound like you? Do you have a chip on your shoulder? But the real question is, are you willing to run through a wall to succeed? Do you have what it takes? Well then, it's my honor to be the first to welcome you to *Walk On Island*. This book is for you.

We All Face Adversity

I believe how long life holds us down is not a matter of circumstance or where you start, but rather a combination of your mindset, determination, grit, and maybe even a bit of luck.

We all have seasons that we know and recognize in our lives. Football season was my favorite, but then there was basketball season and other sports seasons that I also enjoyed. Many times we think of weather seasons, which I also enjoyed. We often think of weather seasons, such as winter, spring, summer, and fall. Again, you can think of them as particular periods in life: childhood, teen years, young adult, etc.

I'll give you some examples that you will come across throughout your life. Some you've experienced before, and some you will see as you move through life. Seasons of elementary school, middle school, high school, college, career, business, religion, relationships, and family. You will constantly be transitioning in and out of those seasons and moving on to the next and next season. No person is exempt.

The bottom line is, you can't avoid adversity. You must work with it and through it because it will never go away. It's always right there in the morning when you wake up. If you can't own up to life's struggles, you aren't prepared to overcome the adversity we will most certainly face. You have to believe you can overcome it; you have to be prepared, ready for change, and ready to go to work.

Having a Winning Season

Every season presents new challenges, but I believe we are defined by the mentality that determines how we approach those challenges. That mentality also shapes our planning, strategy, and actions as we successfully work our way through the season.

At the end of the day, we only get a limited number of seasons before kicking the bucket. I, *Terrell Douglas*, believe we must make the most of every single one of those seasons. Therefore, we must tackle each challenge to win the season. To have the best life possible, we must do our best to stack up multiple winning seasons.

This book will give you the blueprint to the mindset that I built from facing half a lifetime's worth of challenges. That blueprint is what I have affectionately named *Walk On Island*. I use the term "Island" to represent a challenge that you're facing in your life. I have learned that succeeding in life comes down to how you receive, accept, approach, face, adapt and take action to remedy the many challenges that come your way.

Where is Walk-on Island?

"Walk-On Island" was technically a physical location, but more so, Walk-On Island was a place of legends. The many people who earned the right to be there are names you probably haven't heard of. For the walk-on student-athletes at the University of Houston football program, this was where our lockers were located. We'll talk more about that later.

It now physically does not exist, but it still lives in the minds of the men whose cleats touched the floor of that sacred ground as a representation of a particular mindset.

Honestly, it took me a long time to identify I was walking through these islands, and I had to use this certain mentality throughout my life to make it. Now I can recognize it clear as day, and I want to teach you to take that mindset into every facet of your life, own your challenges, your islands, and truly find success in your life.

What is the Walk-on Island Mentality?

Most of the time, people mention being a walk-on as more of a negative connotation describing a person who could not make the team by merit, lacking talent or experience. College football taught me the value of being a "walk-on."

My version of being a walk-on in principle stems more from the mentality standpoint than its label. Throughout my life, I have given it a name, "The Walk-on Island Mentality." The mentality is that drive, or more so that laser focus, what you might identify as, that "Mamba Mentality," which activates even when minimum opportunities are given to prove yourself other than just showing up for practice and making the team. Not all of us can envision ourselves as one of the all-time greats like Kobe, but we can definitely strive for more success in our lives.

I've been on many journeys that I have had to activate this mentality. Whether it was with the church, football, family, or even my current season as a musician, I have had to grind through the muck and get it done. No excuses! The hardships in our lives make us protective of the important things.

I picture the walk-on mentality as an island because it brings up the image of making your way. Sometimes we may find ourselves alone. Other times we find ourselves with a colleague or a friend on various islands throughout life; places where we must figure out solutions. This is when the Walk-on Island mentality kicks in. My season now is to focus on my family and ensure they are physically, spiritually, emotionally, and financially cared for. It can be considered an island because the determination to make sure that my wife and daughter keep a healthy and joyful lifestyle will be consistently met with obstacles in which the Walk-On Island mentality will most definitely be needed.

So you're wondering, what is *Walk On Island?* What does it mean? How does this apply to me? How do I use it?

The Blueprint

What are the principles of Walk on Island Mentality?

Be Optimistic: Optimism comes when you have a vision for a brighter future for yourself. Understand that you can do it if you take it one day and one moment at a time. When you fail, get back up and see yourself getting better. Realize that tomorrow can be a better day if you intentionally make it better, one positive action at a time compounded over and over again. See it and believe in it!

Be Prepared: Refuse to be caught off guard by adversity; expect it and prepare for it. Commit to taking on the challenges that life presents. Be willing to put in the time and effort it takes to improve every situation. Prepare mentally, spiritually, in your relationships, and for your job. Your ability to prepare will be the key to taking advantage of opportunities as they present themselves. Plan, strategize and build your future. Others that see your passion will be there to pick you up when you need it most.

Be Flexible: You must be willing to adjust. Accept feedback and learn from it. When something goes wrong, adjust your plan and move in a new direction quickly. Know yourself and be true to yourself, but allow yourself to be humble. The more you know, the more you realize that you don't know shit. Understand and be able to accept constructive criticism which will help you along your journey. Understand that change will happen, life is hard, and adversity will present itself at every turn. Your flexibility determines how quickly you can pivot when something goes wrong.

Be Relentless: This means you must be intentional, disciplined, and meticulous. Never give up, stop, or be distracted. Stay focused. Be okay with taking two steps forward and one step back, but know that by continuing to push forward and drive your feet, no one can stop you. Success is for the gritty people who refuse to give up.

My Story

This book isn't an autobiography. It's an attempt to show how my life and circumstances formed my way of thinking and shaped my future outlook. My story is a path forward for anyone struggling with life and the failures and challenges we face and wish to overcome. The purpose of this book is to encourage you to develop your own *Walk-on Island* Mentality. Within each chapter, I will illustrate a different challenge I faced and how I met the challenges head-on.

Thomas Edison tried hundreds of materials and thousands of ways to make the first light bulb, but he never said those attempts were failures. What he did say was, "I have not failed 10,000 times. I have not failed once. I have succeeded in proving that those 10,000 ways will not work."

I have also missed the mark and come up short 10,000 times, but similarly, I haven't failed either. I've had to adapt my way of thinking and doing things to succeed. You can do the same if you choose to. How? By learning from some of my mistakes and applying this formula to your own life.

Follow my lead and overcome the burdens and obstacles of life and grow happy, healthy, and successful!

Island Genesis

"Are you hurt or injured?"
-Most of my coaches

R ememering my early life is like holding a handful of puzzle pieces. I know what I'm viewing isn't everything that happened, and even now, I can't fit the pieces together well enough to form the kind of pictures I'd like, but it's what I've got.

My family bounced around small-town Texas for many of my early years. I'm not sure if my mother was chasing my father, or they were chasing down work, but our family grew from one child to three. I was the youngest, but it did not stop me from leading. Don't get me wrong—it's not that my siblings were weak or willing to take a back seat, but I liked being the leader. I wasn't cocky, but I knew what I knew, and it was enough for me to speak my mind when I needed to.

My parents were steadily poor, struggling with the bills a young family gets saddled with in the Great State of Texas. They did what they could to keep a roof over our heads while my brother, sister, and I adapted quickly to new neighborhoods, new apartments, and new friends. At a young age, I learned that friends could carry you a long way if you choose wisely, even if you lose touch from time to time. That's because you can't lose real friends, only phonies. Friends pick you up, talk to you honestly, and listen when you need an ear. Even now, as I said, I try to choose wisely.

So, I've been lucky over the years with many of the friends I've made. We've talked, argued, gotten angry with each other, but if you keep a dialogue going, you can learn and grow with each other. People aren't that different from one another. **Keep the ones that prop you up and lose the ones that suck the life out of you.**

As for my family, it never occurred to me that we were any different from anyone else, but oh, how we moved, usually, when the rent was due.

We took along a favorite toy or two, played ball in the dying grass of a dozen apartment courtyards and the streets while my sister stayed inside playing dress-up with her dolls. We went to school when we had to until the hot months of summer came.

Often, that brought another move because my father took to ghosting us on Fridays. Friday was payday, and it didn't matter whether we were in Everman, TX, or the Highland Hills complex of Fort Worth; my dad liked drugs. They gnawed at him like rats on cheese and wouldn't let loose. He went to town on weekends with his cash, our cash, our rent money. So more often than not, we'd go to another apartment down the road, far enough away that we could find a place, anyplace, to lay our heads.

We didn't have the stability like the kids I went to school with because who knew how long we'd stay? I don't even think my folks did. Changes came around fast, and we leaned on each other to get by.

Somehow, Momma always made it happen, even if she found us just a single room to sleep in with a few thin blankets on the floor. We called it a pallet out in the country and made do with what we had. She had a remarkable ability to make it interesting—fun, even while we were living without most of life's luxuries.

When she came across a little money, she bought us an air mattress. It was better than the hard floor. Later, the air mattress became an actual mattress on the floor when Momma found a deal at the T-Mart swap-meet nearby. Momma didn't have enough money for the box springs or bed frame, but it was a real mattress we were sharing, all four of us.

Now we had some luxury: a mattress. It was great, even when I got elbowed, kicked, or rolled onto the floor and thumped my head. I would wake up, push my way back into the warmth of the bed, and get some sleep. Momma made sure there was a little something to eat. I won't say I went to bed hungry too often, but most nights, I could have eaten more.

Big Mamma Bunt (my mother's mom) always said, "You best be happy with what you got and work for what you want," so I learned to manage what I had and tried not to wish for more food.

Grimy Island

"We must accept finite disappointment,
but never lose infinite hope."
            -Martin Luther King, Jr.

When I was about four, we were in Everman, Texas. My mother's sister lived there, and with my dad somewhere in the outback, we needed a place to stay. Shocking, I know. My mother worked at a grocery store, "moving boxes," as she said, trying to keep our financial heads above water.

That left us with our aunt and her daughter in the mornings. When my aunt had work, mom was home, or a girl from down the street stayed with us for a few hours.

I remember she was twelve years old and skinny. One of my puzzle pieces shows me her face, but somehow, I thought her name was Bree. Maybe it was Brittany, but when you're four, most of your gumballs are still stacked up in the machine.

What I do remember is she could read. That was a precious commodity since we didn't have a TV, so we got stories when it got too dark to play outside. It probably drove her crazy, pestering her all the time, but she always gave in eventually. She might have been reading from *National Geographic*, *Ebony*, or her schoolwork, and it didn't matter; we liked the attention, and we liked her voice.

What I didn't like was when my dad came to the house and acted like he hadn't been gone for weeks. I'm not sure if he came around one day and talked my mother into giving him another chance, or if my aunt decided she'd had enough of his big talk and little support, but we moved again.

Our stay in Everman, Texas, was neither long nor profitable, and we found ourselves in such familiar territory that my mother would stand over the kitchen sink doing the same dishes over and over. I think she did that so we wouldn't know she was crying, but our dinner dishes got real clean every night.

What changed her mind, I don't know, but after years of moving around, my mother said we should move back into my great-grandmothers's house. Big Mamma Lillian had passed several years earlier, and the little house stood vacant. The front yard was a disaster, with weeds and dry dirt. The back yard was worse.

The house itself was a brick and wood home in Mansfield, Texas, below Dallas and Fort Worth. I had been there before and had a vague early memory of the place, but it looked different when we returned. The years hadn't been kind, and things were falling apart.

Momma gave my sister, and brother, and me tasks to do as we moved in with our few belongings. We ducked as many of them as we could, but the spider-infested place needed help. There were thick cobwebs everywhere, chips in the paint, windows that wouldn't shut right because the building was sagging into the foundation, and lots of dust and grime.

If you don't know Texas, the state is a great melting pot of this and that, yin and yang. There's a lot of push and shove between ranchers and city folk, small towns and big, and Friday night football dominates the talk in every barbershop and diner.

Maybe "dominates" isn't the right word. It's not strong enough. The town folks are fanatics. Any rule could be bent and twisted like a pretzel if it helped one team over another. Neighboring towns recruit players when they are just kids in junior high. Payoffs happen, and I remember hearing about a seriously crazy lady who tried to hire a killer to hit the mother of her daughter's cheerleading rival. Yes, even the cheerleading squads are coveted spots.

Have you ever heard of *Friday Night Lights*? The movie and the series are fiction, but that doesn't mean the premise isn't true. And I'd like to go on record saying the stories were tame compared to the real thing. People live and die for their high school football in Texas.

Returning to Mansfield meant my father made another attempt to be back in our lives. He'd be fine for a few days, and then we'd catch him asleep in the car, parked haphazardly across the rutted driveway as we walked to school in the early morning. Other times he'd leave on Friday payday and come back on Monday, half high, half manic, to see if Momma had any money left.

That usually precipitated a little conversation, which turned into a screaming match. Fighting seemed like the most natural thing in the world since I heard the harsh words and constant arguing. Those times usually ended with Dad leaving.

He'd wait for the perfect moment then he would sneak off with the car. When he did, we had no way to get to the grocery store for food. Usually, that didn't matter too much because if Momma hadn't been able to hide her purse before he showed up, there was no cash left anyway. If he couldn't find her purse, we'd soon be missing something we needed because he would pawn it for his next fix.

As my parent's relationship strained and cracked at the foundation, so did the old house. Giant spiders crawled through numerous holes in the walls and scuttled across the floor. I could hear the larger ones, the wolf spiders when they jumped to attack insects and smaller spiders.

One of my happiest times was when we got a real bed, a metal frame, and box springs to sleep in and got off the floor. Still, there were plenty of nights when I saw things crawling across the ceiling, and I had to roll over and cover my head. That helped, but it couldn't drown out the sounds of little feet. Rat feet. The kind with nails that scratched and skittered across the hard floors and rustled in and out of the walls. The kind that gnawed at the edges of my mattress when it sat on the ground. I loved my bed frame and box springs.

If that sounds horrible, it's only a fragment of what was moving in and out of our home. As the house disintegrated, stray animals forced their way in and wandered around. We had to get stones and sticks from the backyard to keep the cats out. Once that was done, the pipes burst, and we had no water. No money, no plumber, just family.

The house was crumbling like a giant sandcastle, but dad was out doing who knows what, and there was no way to get anything fixed. Without plumbing, we took to filling gallon jugs with water from a hose across the street from where we stayed.

Hauling those jugs got us enough water to cook with when there was food in the pantry, but washing and taking a bath was another story. The bathtub was way too big to fill a gallon at a time, so we used small tubs to take sits-baths. It was tolerable. Not having a working toilet wasn't.

I had to find relief in the backyard and wipe with leaves or grass since there wasn't any toilet paper. The water thing started to get to me, physically and mentally. It seemed so unfair, and going through that unfairness made me see actual fairness as an illusion. It was a reality for others, but not for me.

When you face adversity, especially at a young age, it makes you tough or a victim. I'm not a victim; I'm a realist. And, I'm built for endurance. I don't put up with things like that anymore; I don't endure them; I fix them. But at a young age, you've got to take things as they come. I learned early I would need to be prepared for whatever happened. We all needed to survive.

Musician Island

"For every dark night, there's a brighter day."

-*Tupac*

For quite a while, the water in our house came from an abandoned building across the street; but the comfort the church across the street provided was much more than that. It was an outlet, a meeting place, and an inspiration that drew me to its doors multiple times a week. I was young and hadn't yet realized that my father's comings and goings weren't normal. Our unstable home was all I knew, so it was normal to my way of thinking, but it was tough.

When my Dad was around, he'd work when he could. If he were home, my folks would fight, night after night. It gave him a reason to leave, which was likely his plan anyway. Fueling his jealousy and addiction we'd notice something missing like a box fan, window air conditioning unit, or a space heater by the following day.

We went without air conditioning for many summers because Daddy had taken away our window AC unit and sold it for drugs. He would take anything of value with him when he went, including our spirit. One winter, he took a whole Christmas from us.

That Christmas, the once abundant Christmas tree, now had just a few gifts underneath. I looked over to where the rest of my family stood. My mother, bless her soul, smiled at me, but the light did not quite reach her eyes. My sister's tear-stained face told me she had been crying. My brother just watched my mother, and the frown on his face told me he wasn't happy. Every gift that was under the tree had vanished and been replaced by two or three convenience store toys by my drained teary-eyed mother. My daddy ruined this Christmas. For me, I just wanted to make sure my mother was okay. Consoling her was more important than anything else. I still think to this day, how my mom rushed to an open convenience store to buy a few things to make sure that we were able to open something that morning.

Daddy being there and then gone was a constant in my life. That and having a big hole in the window frame where our latest air conditioner used to be. The other constant was the church, and since my mother has sixteen brothers and sisters, we had plenty of family around.

The church across the street was an inspiration. In Momma's world, everyone had to go to church. My grandfather was a minister, and although he was small in stature, he stood tall in his word. Papa Eugene and Big Momma Bunt would make sure to have all sixteen of their children in attendance religiously, pun intended. Not only did we have to be there, but they were responsible for keeping order for whatever role they would volunteer for. At one point, the Wilson/Lawson family were the only children of the Bethlehem Missionary Baptist Church, aside from a few others, and led district competitions with other churches. When old enough, all sixteen sung in the choir, and while two of the six boys went on to serve in our military, the other four followed in their father's lineage to become ministers. The ladies grew to be leaders in the church while also earning degrees and raising their families.

We all had to sing in the choir. My Momma has a beautiful voice and eventually led as their director for quite a while. This is where I took on my love for music, but my area was always beside the organ on the drums. I took to being there three or four times a week, more than a Pastor's kid in a lot of places. Monday, Tuesday, Thursday, and some Saturdays were the days that I was there. Then sunrise church service at 8 am, Sunday school, and finally, the main church service at 11 am.

That's where I first remember intentionally applying the walk-on island mentality. I wasn't initially aware of the discipline needed to grow into an effective musician, but as I started *Musician Island*, I began to build a work ethic, refusing to give up or be distracted. *Musician Island* would be a place I would revisit throughout my life.

By nine, I was trading songs with my three cousins Chaz, Thomas, and Andrew. Thomas and I were the least experienced of our lot, but we had passion. My cousin Marcus taught us the fundamentals of drumming, and since I was young and the others were a lot better than me, I had to fight for opportunities to play.

When othres would disrespect me, or accuse me of not staying on the beat, or even that I sucked, I was not discouraged. Instead, it stirred my natural competitiveness, and drove me to practice relentlessly until I could play better than my cousins.

Anytime I could sneak my way to the empty drums (and sometimes even when someone else was playing), I'd practice everything. I didn't have a metronome to practice with, but got good at timekeeping, and I'd go from simple left-right, left-right single strokes to double strokes, and paradiddles, which was a beat you play with the drums. I transferred this practice and strong mind work ethic for sports and sports practice.

Every Sunday after services, we would gather with twelve of the seventeen brothers and sisters that still lived in town. There was room to play outside the church, and our house was right across the street. That gave us lots of time to mingle, play, and catch up on what had happened in the last week or so. That familiarity grounded me, gave me a place, and gave us plenty of time together to help and heal whatever was weighing us down. Often, it was Daddy.

I was always the smallest apple in the bunch, but my bite was bigger than my bark. Daddy called me the runt of the family. It was tough being the smallest in my grade, but in the sports realm, I excelled. Where a closed mind saw only disadvantage or adversity, I saw an opportunity, and I was able to take advantage of it using my size. I stayed focused on pushing forward and driving toward my goals.

Opponents underestimated my drive and my talent. When they dismissed me or refused to see me as a threat, I surprised them with my speed, power, and agility. I took a lot of satisfaction in teaching them that not choosing me for their team in pickup games was a big mistake.

I wasn't very good at trading insults, but Momma was a fighter, and she didn't raise any soft children. I didn't consider myself a fighter, physically, since she pressed us never to pass the first lick. But she did say that if someone took a swing at us, then it was on. She said, "Don't start no fights, but if they swing, you better finish it."

Momma's way of teaching helped me face and beat (no pun intended) adversity. Daddy echoed those practices while adding, "Never give up on your goals."

Nelson Mandela said, "Education is the most powerful weapon you can use to change the world," and like him, our family believed in learning. Sixteen of the seventeen kids in Momma's family graduated from Mansfield High School and had roles in the church. I'd say Bib Momma and Paw had to be relentless to raise a household of children with those morals through and through.

Bastard Island

"You might not have a car or big gold chain; stay true to yourself, and things will change."

- Snoop Dogg

Although Daddy always seemed to show up regularly, his returns became less often. His habits were terrible, but they helped prepare me for what life could throw my way. I learned that preparation was essential, whether mentally or spiritually, for whatever the next island presented.

With Daddy out of the picture, our home and the financial situation got slightly better, but it was still shaky. If I looked out the window and saw the power truck, I figured we were in for a cold night. That fear was constant but lessened as we refused to be caught off guard.

One of my mother's younger sisters was also struggling, and she moved in with us. The house had three bedrooms, so my mother, sister, brother, and I squeezed into one bedroom while my aunt and my cousins squeezed into the other. Then, our two families' worth of belongings got mashed together into the house's other room. Yes, it was a mess.

Sharing a room was comforting in a way, but we spent a lot of time in the living room or playing outside. That's where I felt best. I could spread out, run till I dropped, play football, or have WWE wrestling matches with my cousins and friends. So, close quarters or not, we worked things out.

My mother's sisters and brothers would sit together to have random meetings, but as a fly on the wall, I never heard specific strategies for how anyone would help the other.

Our situation did take care of some issues like babysitting, cooking, and cleaning. Both sisters wanted the best for their children, but they never communicated how much they wanted each other to thrive. I grew up seeing this trait in my other aunts and uncles, too—a good lesson for me as I grew older, to tell others how I felt.

Still, it was a blessing to have loved ones around for playtime, and we had the opportunity to build an uncompromising bond. And then, amid this new family melding, my world's biggest curveball was thrown at me by the one I trusted the most. I never saw it coming.

I was five when my mother sat me down and told me that the only man I knew and shared my last name with was not my biological father. Later in life, one of my mentors, Ben Adkins, told me, "Whenever your capacity of learning is only eight ounces, I can't pour a gallon's worth of information in at one time. Your brain is not prepared to take in that much information. I have to allow you to drink from the eight ounces before I can add anything else." Well, this seemed like one of those overflowing moments that may have been a little complex for a five-year-old's eight-ounce glass.

As I looked at her, my mind went foggy, like a mist that rises above a lake and blocks away the sun, had come into our living room to stay. I vaguely remember what she said to me and remember even less about my first meeting with this stranger. The world had split open, and I was on one side of the chasm, and everyone else was on the other.

After that, any guy that came around my family or talked to my mother was unacceptable by my standards. I ain't let nobody make it. As soon as I saw them, my blood began to boil.

At school, I would hear kids talk about all of the fun their families had on outings and vacations, and I thought, *that's how every household should be.* I had only known one man as my father and planned on keeping that relationship – as shaky as it was at times – the way it was.

There isn't a pattern or anything I could see from my mother dating new guys other than my dad, and I never gave them a chance. I often used my preparation and relentless "walk-on island mentality" for wrong doing. Around nine years old, my folks split for the 25th time. My mother began to date, and I wasn't having it. If a man showed up at the house, I would break his car windows and lights with rocks, branches, or anything else I could find without missing a beat. I would flatten their tires and try to do whatever it took not to have anyone at the house. When I couldn't get my way, I would run away from home, at least until I got hungry or sleepy.

Like clockwork, Daddy would still appear when my mother's paycheck would clear, and she'd have some cash, or worse yet, there'd be a new TV or something else he could drag away to the pawnshop to satisfy his jealousy and drug habit.

I recall crying in disbelief. When the man came to visit, I denied him so much as eye contact. I wished against all hope that he would say that it wasn't true, just a mistake or a joke. But that didn't happen. So, I began to build an imaginary wall with any male that had not already established a worthy relationship with me. Why wouldn't I? Who could I trust now for a fair shake?

There's a lot of stubbornness in my family, and I carry that trait. Still, I heard things at church that eased my mind just a bit. My family coached me about creating an opportunity to at least allow my biological father to have some open communication with me. He had been absent so long, but that could change if I gave him a chance. At first, I thought, *so what?* He'd been gone so long, and I wasn't a kid; I was growing up. Where the hell had he been?

I thought about letting him in just a little. I'd mull over the possibilities as I played drum riffs at church, working till the sticks were a part of my hands, a part of me. My father was a part of me, no matter what I felt, and eventually, I gave him a chance to be in my life. I learned that he had once tried to do small things for me earlier in my life, but he quit. Gave up, couldn't be bothered to be persistent or regular—his loss.

I know now that he was in the military, but I have no idea why he got out. Our conversations never got that far. He was there, and then once again, he was gone. I tried reaching out to him on multiple occasions, but our relationship never stabilized. He never became a staple in my life.

On the other hand, the drums were a big part of my life, and when my cousins moved on, I became the unpaid main drummer at the church. I was 12 when my musical acumen got stronger, tighter, and I gained a lot of confidence, having been counted on to be there and to be sharp. When I wasn't drumming, I was playing sports with a vengeance and exhaustion.

On the basketball court, I was fast and loved to anticipate when someone was about to make a pass I could get to. I didn't care if I had to dive for the ball across the court or into the stands; I was stopping or stealing the pass.

When I wasn't grabbing a pass, I would guard the best player on the opposing team. I didn't care how big they were; it didn't matter. If they were the biggest threat, then I was on them. I covered them like a blanket. The challenge was there, and I needed to beat it.

When I wasn't shooting hoops, there were plenty of other sports. I started running track to burn some of my excess energy. I found speed I never knew I had and beat the fastest kids at school in races. If they were ahead near the end of the race, I drew from deep-down and bolted past them to win.

Academically, I was slightly above average at a young age. I loved and hated school all at the same time. I didn't have a hard time creating relationships, but it was sometimes difficult to keep friends. My mother taught me to be kind even if someone wasn't kind to me, which often happened since I was in a predominantly white school district. There were times where I would get blamed for something

I didn't do or know about. Now, those memories aren't too memorable.

In elementary school, Momma did what she could to send me off to school, put together. Whatever Momma made at work didn't include enough for our family to dress in the newest or best clothes. My appearance wasn't important to me at the time, and Momma tried, but I didn't make it home the way she sent me most of the time. Me being a boy showed through my actions as a challenge to see how dirty I could get.

I had holes in my jeans and shirts because we used a barbed wire fence to dry our clothes, and I had accidents at school, causing students to call me names. So yes, I was the stinky kid. This label was a tough one to shake, especially when you try to cover it up and one of your closest friends is the loudest in the school who does anything for laughs. David, one of my best friends to this day, became a consistent thorn in my thumb. He kept me on my toes and held me accountable in a couple of stories worth addressing in upcoming chapters.

Still, I weathered the storms, even when I had to lie about my living conditions occasionally to keep myself in school. One time my teacher asked about my bag's smell. Instead of telling her the truth, I told her I accidentally dropped it in a puddle or something along those lines.

Sometimes it seemed like the madness never stopped. Dealing with my issues at home and the bullying at school, a lot of the time from David, was a one-two punch that left me dizzy and against the ropes almost every day. But I'd still drag myself out of bed every morning and keep on getting on. Sometimes I'd hear my grandfather Eugene Wilson saying, "Right is right, and right don't wrong nobody," and I'd know kids would be kids, jerks sometimes, so I promised myself I wouldn't bully or degrade others. In the moments that life's challenges occur, I'd put forth the time and effort to improve any situation.

Island Degradation

"We must build dikes of courage to hold
back the flood of fear."
          – Martin Luther King, Jr.

I was a church boy at heart. Whenever I wasn't at school or a church service, my cousins, friends, and I would find our way across the street to the church to play basketball, football, rollerblade, and ride bikes. My mother worked long hours as the Deli Manager at Albertson's, and we did our best to stay busy. Still, with all those opportunities, I was able to find ways to get in some type of trouble.

    My friends and I were looking for innocent fun, but an idle mind is the devil's playground. Growing boys are usually only thinking of having fun and eating. It's the way it is. There were days when we got a little impatient and took matters into our own hands and found ways to find food or money for food. This was another one of the many times that my preparation was used inefficiently.

One of our best plans was to go to each of our homes and scrounge for food and then rummage around in drawers, chairs, and couches for nickels and dimes. Then we got a little bolder and broke into other people's houses and dug in their couches and drawers for food money. That was all well and good for a while, but we were knuckleheads and started thinking it was normal to break in and take any money we could find.

I'm not sure what triggered that thinking or why I did it, but we weren't as smart as we thought we were. It didn't take long for the police to catch us, and we all got busted. We got a slap on the wrist since we were minors, and there were no charges filed for breaking and entering. We were successful in most of these trips, but that energy could have been angled toward more positive ways to make money. Given the climate, it's a blessing that we weren't shot and killed by a homeowner or a police officer.

This leads me to a real consequence when funny ideas happen, allowing the opportunity for poor preparation and lack of flexibility to meet like one of my hilarious "stinky kid" moments.

I recall the day of a math test my seventh-grade year. Usually, when someone starts a sentence with, "what had happened was...", they are about to lie. But in this case, I'll keep it one hunnit.

I had the bubble guts or needed to poop for the simple minds, and my teacher wouldn't allow me restroom privilege before we began our test. Again, "what had happened was..." I thought it would be funny for me to rip a silent but deadly, but man did that backfire, in the literal sense. The fart started nice and airy, but at the tail end, it felt like I was two and a half centimeters dialated. I finished my test by marking in a bunch of random answers, turned in my test, then ran straight to the locker room like John Witherspoon as Pops in the movie *Next Friday*.

The embarrassment could have ended there, but I forgot that the entire football team would soon be walking into the locker room. Here's where a quick pivot could have minimized a mishap. Instead of trying to hide the newly created bicycle streak, I magnified the situation by removing my favorite pair of white boxer underwear and putting them into the toilet. But wait, there's more... The commode wouldn't flush. I panicked and quickly left the restroom area of the locker room full of athletes getting ready for practice. I should've left it alone, but then I became a part of the search team, picking up and throwing around the underwear, trying to see who the culprit was.

Boy, did I get roasted for that, but the situation had no bearing on what was to come. A few lessons learned in this situation was to not make a big deal out of something small and to own up to your actions, and to know yourself through the consequences of your situation. I thought that was bad enough; then a definite life-changing moment came to a head. This would cause me to leave the school district for a year and get a new approach to my future.

Another day at school, a buddy of mine called me over at lunchtime. "Take a look at this, T. I got it this weekend at the swap meet."

"What is it?" I asked. But he just smiled and showed me a burnished butterfly knife.

"Man, that's cool," was all I had. I was so impressed.

"Sweet, huh? Watch this, as he flips and twists the knife. Look how sharp it is. Cuts like a razor. Ain't nobody gonna mess with me when I've got this."

"Man, that's what's up—let me get that up off you. Loan it to me, let me at least get it the rest of the week? I'm just trying to learn them tricks."

"No way, man. Just got it," my friend said.

"Yo, just let me take it home tonight, big dawg."

"Aight, man, but bring it back tomorrow. You owe me," he said.

I owed him alright. The first thing that happened was I took the knife home and carefully kept it out of sight. I didn't want my mother to find it. That would be bad, so I was careful. I thought I was careful when I brought it to school the next day, too. Middle school. Thirteen years old.

It was like my teacher had x-ray vision or something. I somehow managed to get caught with a felony-length blade in middle school. I lied to my mom and told her that someone put it in my bag because I didn't want to disappoint her. Then I thought about it and decided not to lie to the cops about having it on me when they pulled me out of class, which is why they didn't have me arrested and escorted off the premises in handcuffs.

With the hard grip of the police officer's hand, I didn't feel anything but numb. I can't say that I was scared, but I was more nervous about disappointing my mom. So it was a step in the right direction, as far as being accountable and telling the cops, but It still sucked. Had I lied, I possibly would have taken the walk of shame in cuffs and been shipped straight to the juvenile detention center. Lukily, for me, they let my mom pick me up.

The look in my mother's eyes had me feeling like I had let her down, ashamed for what I did. I also was disappointed in myself when I realized what I did was wrong. I have gone down the wrong path.

Mom had to take me to the juvenile detention center for booking. I never ratted my friend out, and he was pissed because the principal took the knife and never gave it back. What I got was probation, and it didn't seem too bad at the time. I saw my mother crying, and the look of disappointment on her face was devastating. Right then, I vowed to her that I would straighten up and graduate college. At that point, I had been humbled and pledged to be true to myself.

After that, my friends and I spent most of our time playing ball at church or in school sports. No more knives. Live and learn.

Not too long after, the church decided I should get paid for my drum work, and after every Sunday service, I got $50 for my part in the music. I took a lot of pride in getting paid to be a musician. Applying the walk-on island preparation, flexibility, and relentless attitude, all those years of practice paid off, even if the first time I picked those sticks up, I had been terrible.

During the coming year, I started to excel at football by playing pick games and "throw up tackle" with my older family and friends.

In my adolescence, I received a scholarship to attend Emmitt Smith's football camp one summer. Smith was the star running back for the Dallas Cowboys and became the NFL's all-time leading rusher in 2002, which was a big endorsement of my talent. I had been playing running back, and I was excelling. I had speed, and I could slip tacklers like they were playing flag football. I was said to be the GOAT in the Pop Warner realm by some. But these talents didn't transfer as I aged, like is the case with early bloomed athletes.

This was when my relationship with my homie Greg and London begin to solidify. These two were solid athletes. Greg's height rose to match his multisport abilities. He had the opportunities to develop in sports other than just football and basketball. London was just a gifted individual. I felt that there wasn't anything he couldn't do on or off the field. I would say in many ways; he was the most overall athletic of the bunch. Greg would say otherwise, but that's Greg. You had to show him, and he would say and do anything to prove you wrong. David was always the strongest, while a buddy, Duane and I, were the runts of the group.

Still, it wasn't all perfect. I almost quit playing ball in high school, but a long-overdue growth spurt finally kicked in, and I gained six inches in height. This was when Darius and I became good friends. Darius wasn't very athletic looking, but way more talented than he received credit for, mainly due to his quiet demeanor and nonchalant personality. My physical growth made a massive difference on the field. Instead of being a hindrance to the team, I became an asset wherever I was needed though I wasn't given the option of being a varsity player until junior year. It was one of those play on JV or ride the bench on Varsity situations.

I had talent on both offensive and defensive sides of the ball, but I was more comfortable carrying the ball on offense. Due to injuries junior year, I got to carry the ball the last few games on Thursday night instead of riding the bench as a varsity linebacker during Friday night lights. There were games in which I totally demolished defensive players running the ball. I scored a few touchdowns, but all in all, I had exceptional games as a running back and thought that was helping to seal my fate as a respected athlete on the team.

I also began to take my grades a bit more seriously. I did well on the field and hit the books almost as hard as I worked on the field. Alright, that's an exaggeration. I played football like there was no tomorrow. But I did good enough in my classes. My GPA had to be decent enough for me to stay on the team, and it had to be worthy enough to get me into college. I honestly didn't know what good enough for college meant. I just thought it meant I had to pass, and that was enough. It meant I had to keep up my grades. With this, I moved in with my aunt and her kids until I graduated.

I was still looking at going to college, and in the middle of all that, Jasmine, my childhood sweetheart and I decided to date. I knew she had a great chance at eventually becoming my wife. She was beautiful, intelligent, and her selfless demeanor was what drew me in like a moth to a flame. She was beautiful, both inside and outside. What a year I was having.

I still had trust issues, especially with men, but after overcoming a long series of relationship issues and home struggles, I started feeling like I could be successful. Meeting and overcoming adversity was now a possibility. Nothing seemed insurmountable anymore. I saw adversity as a challenge, something I could face head-on and know I had a fighting chance.

My blueprint moment came when I realized there was a higher future out there in the distance. I drew optimism from that vision. Tomorrow was going to be better if I intentionally made it that way, and saw myself succeeding.

In the off-season, I worked in the weight room religiously, doing extended sessions of set after set of heavy lifting. It strengthened my core and added even more muscle to my thighs, which helped me get that first blast of speed I needed against my opponents. I was five-foot-eight as a senior, playing at a hundred and eighty-three pounds.

We had some excellent coaches, and they drove us through two-a-day practices in the late summer heat of Texas. It didn't make us the best team in the county, but we were competitive. The harder I worked, the better I got, and although my coaches changed my position and it was the first time I'd ever played the defensive line, I received district honors and was our team MVP at the defensive end position.

I hated D-line. As a matter of fact, I hated being on the line so much that I wrote a paper about it. It started with "Running down to the fieldhouse..." It was trash and my homie John let me know that, off the top. With what I had accomplished in a small-scale JV game, I still figured that I had done enough to be taken more seriously than to have my hand put in the dirt.

John and I became friends at the end of my junior and senior years. I had a great year as a junior on JV playing both sides of the ball. As embarrassed as I felt, one of my buddies, Stephan Taylor, told me "you can only control what you can control." My job was to play like a man amongst boys with the hope of being given an opportunity to run the ball my senior season. Based on my junior year of running the ball, I would have racked up some pretty impressive stats on varsity. Running back is more of a glory position. You took a lot of punishment, but you noticed that you were carrying the ball and scoring touchdowns. With that, I wouldn't have had to worry about being recognized at all. I would've been needed.

I waited impatiently the last few weeks of the season for contact with the college scouts I hoped were in the stands. I knew they were up there watching games sometimes, so I kept waiting. Mansfield high school wasn't exactly a hotbed of talent my senior season, but we got some local press. I had to wait and see if that was enough to get those scouts into the stands. I needed to get a full-ride scholarship to college, and after the year I had, there was that chance.

Once the football season ended, my hope faded; I should l have had some good contact with at least the small Texas colleges, but no offers came as the school year dragged on. I had good grades and okay scores on my ACT, but changing positions from offense to defensive line probably killed my chances. College coaches get dazzled by guys who play three years of varsity and amass huge running stats or break county or state records for tackles. I didn't have that resume to get the press to generate interest.

My high school career ended the way it started without much fanfare. What college was going to pick up an undersized one-year varsity D-lineman? I hit summertime without hope or a college commitment. It hit me like a ton of bricks.

Still, as strange as it might seem, against all hope (and sense), the events comented my belief in optiminism, at least in the way things eventually unfolded. If you take anything away from my situation, it is the one positive action at a time compounded over and over that can keep you driven and optimistic. You can see it and believe in it!

Homeless Island

"For some, football is something you play.
For me, football is something I live."
                                        -Terrell Douglas

Before my senior year of football, I dreamed about going to college in the Great State of Texas. I had no plans to live more than an hour from the Dallas-Fort Worth metroplex and thought perhaps I'd go to TCU. If not, my backup was the University of North Texas, about 50 minutes from home. But that didn't happen. No scholarships and I didn't get accepted into the schools where two of my friends were headed. That fueled the wrath that I planned to unleash on the field, but at that point, there was no field.

Summer came and went slowly, filled with despair. My girlfriend and I were at odds most of the time, probably my fault, because I couldn't quite grasp not getting a full-ride scholarship. I'd gone to my classes, gotten good grades, and worked my butt off in practice, which translated into a very good year of high school football, but I had nothing to show for my last three years of work. I didn't get noticed by college coaches, not even Junior College.

My reality wasn't my dream, and instead of finding a college to attend, I moped around town and hung out with friends. Depression is a severe roadblock to anything you want to gain in life. Sometimes I just laid in bed and pretended to be asleep while my mind spun on what was, instead of what could be. I was afraid to move forward. I'd had enough heartache.

I worked out a little, ran some sprints, and tried to cheer myself up, but it wasn't happening. I can't even remember what else I did. Probably nothing good. The summer was a blur.

Fortunately, what I did have were some good friends. Eventually, my buddies, Greg, Darius, David, and I decided to take a road trip to a Junior College in east Texas during winter break for enrollment. First, I had to drag my tail out of bed, and put clothes on. Then I actually had to leave my room. Baby steps. Just getting in the car and heading to the campus was a major leap toward the future. Maybe somewhere out there was a glimmer of hope.

We talked about our prospects in the car, and our goal was to walk-on at the JuCo and earn a football scholarship to a tier-one division four-year school. It's as tough to get noticed at a JuCo as it is in high school, but what choice did we have if we wanted to play ball and get an education?

After walking the campus and checking out the football stadium, I felt my heart beating again after being dormant for so long. We walked and talked and dreamed. Eventually, I was convinced. It was what we needed to do. In the end, two of the four of us, Greg and me, enrolled in the college, and the others moved on with opportunities elsewhere.

We started classes and talked about playing football, but it seemed like I was the one doing all the talking. My friend was wavering, getting disillusioned. My grades were alright, but I had to be honest with myself. Sure, I wanted an education, but football was driving me. I had to try it because I had to know.

Eventually, football rolled around, and I walked on, but my friend did not. I struggled because I hurt my wrist during weight room tryouts before ever even taking the field, but I was charged-up about being ready, and I kept lifting. It got to where I lost feeling in my hand up to my forearm when my palm made contact with anything, but I pushed on. Doing bench-presses became nearly impossible as I strained and compensated for my injury, but I knew that I wouldn't get a chance to show what I could do on the field if I quit. So, I dug in.

We ran a lot of drills daily, hourly, over and over. I'd been running laps for the past month. Staying strong, running sprints, sideways, backward, keeping my footwork strong. That was great, but when practice started, we were mostly just running drills. I was going slightly mad.

When we did finally get to game-style drills, it wasn't as good as I'd hoped. It was tough to hold a football with my hand and wrist injured, much less make the high-point catches. Still, I got short passes during catching drills with few drops, even with my forearm going numb. My legs and coordination were strong; I was a standout in hitting and footwork drills. I tried out for strong and free safety, but there were ten strong safeties and twelve free safeties auditioning. Nearly twenty of them wouldn't make the team.

One of the problems at a junior college is that the coaches often aren't as seasoned as those at a four-year college who have more experience. It's not always a talent thing. Sometimes it is, but often it comes down to them evaluating talent.

Those issues were floating around in the back of my mind as the days of tryouts continued. The JuCo's facilities were okay, but the coaching staff, as I feared, was trash. The offensive coaches were decent and knew their players, but the defense was a mess. There were many days with lots of drills and no plays, no way to prove myself.

My first position coach was a complete imposter who got dumped just after spring ball began.
No joke! A real imposter. Word on the street is that
he was an actual real person claiming to be someone
else, and he had the forged resume to prove it. When
he got fired, I thought things were looking up, but
his replacement was worse. The phoney at least gave
me credit when due, but the new coach insisted on
telling me I was doing drills wrong when I knew I
was mastering it the way better coaches had taught
me. His knowledge of football was mediocre at best.
I mean, the guy couldn't rock as a Pee Wee coach.
One of his favorites would completely miss an as-
signment and still get a pat on the back because the
coach didn't know any better. A perfect example was
how the first team players would mention the plays
with missed assignments and the coach would still
give them a two thumbs up.

We were still drilling and running but getting
game-type situations to prove myself wasn't happening. I knocked a few helmets off, usually because
players took my modest and calm demeanor as
weakness, but it went unnoticed by our replacement
coach. I'm not sure if the other players feared me,
but I wasn't ever hassled; I'd gained their respect.

I wasn't sure about the rest of the coaching staff,
but they had to know I could play. I worked as hard
or harder than anyone every day. Still, there were a
lot of us trying out for the team, and the coaching

change on defense didn't help improve my chances of making the team. The only thing I could hope for was to play well in our upcoming game. I worked every practice with that foremost in my mind, but it wasn't to be.

In the spring game, I got in three plays total. One play was up the middle with the tackle made by a lineman at the line of scrimmage. The second play went to the opposite side for another short gain, and the third was a quick pass to the opposite side of the field. I got to the players just early enough to touch the pile as the tacklers and ball carriers hit the ground. There was nothing for me to do at that point. I'd worked hard and proved myself in practice but had no way to show anything in our game.

There was that wall in my way again. Immense, brutal, and almost impenetrable, but I kept chipping away at it. I'd failed my first goal of making the team, but I refused to quit on my dreams or myself. That night I went to the weight room and worked out, getting ready for an opportunity in the fall. My wrist still throbbed, but I did what I could. I kept running, keeping my mind strong, and doing plenty of sprints.

Toward the end of the semester, I found out that the injury that happened on the second day of weight room training was a dislocation of the lunate bone in my wrist. That was the reason my arm continued to go numb. The bone that popped out of place was at the bottom near the center of the palm of my mind. At the time, I didn't have insurance and afraid of this truth, so I pushed toward my goal at all costs. I sucked it up and kept trying. When I finally saw a doctor in April, he scheduled surgery – four months after I'd dislocated my wrist.

The surgery was successful, but it left me far behind my goal for that time in my life. I had to schedule my doctor's appointments carefully so I wouldn't miss classes, and I also had physical therapy three times each week. Physical therapy is long and painful. Although working with a therapist, it can be a mind-bending, lonely time. Your mind goes off in directions you don't want it drifting. Not to mention wherer the money would come from to pay for therapy.

Once again, the easiest thing to do at that point was to say, "Well, I gave it a shot," and quit. But I had to get my movement back, my hand and finger dexterity, and I still had to know if I could play college ball. Sometimes I saw my surgery, therapy, and recovery as a three-headed monster, but it was a phantom I could beat if I stayed the path. With the doctor saying the results of waiting so long for the surgery caused the tendon damage because it was like stretching a leather belt. It was just another roadblock; it seemed normal. I told myself, *just go forward and find a way around it.*

My buddy Greg and I kept our class schedule and got decent grades, but that second semester was one of the most challenging periods of my college career. With football and the surgery, I didn't think I could take much more, but then I got fired from my job at the church as a percussionist, where I would continue to return as much as I could from the JuCo. I was told that I would be taken off of payroll but not given an explanation as to why.

They didn't know, and maybe I should have said something, but that little gig was my only means of eating. This began to bring about a level of confusion that I had never experienced with my church. I mean, I was there more days than not for a lot of my life, then bam. "This will be your last payroll check," is what I was told at what later became one of my uncle's church.. I'd expect that from the corporate world, but no explanation? It hurt! Even from the leaders of the place I considered sacred.

As soon as the departure happened, it appeared to me that when I went home, I was met with hugs, kisses, and more confusion from there. First, it was my hair. I grew locks for fun, but once my cousin was taken from us, they became more a symbol of appreciation to him. He had taught me a lot about sports, girls, the streets, how to fight, and much more. We had a competition to see whose hair would grow the fastest. He cut his locks just before he was taken from us with multiple gunshot wounds, one fatal.

Again, I didn't know my hair was an issue, but when I found out, I addressed it in what I thought was the proper manner. As I thought, my Pastor and I had a relationship, but I was now being told that I had to follow something called the *chain of command*. I had no idea how this worked at the time, but I guess everyone assumed I did and that I had decided to *buck the system*.

When we knocked out the hair thing, the whole chain of command order was somewhat understood. Not long after I had come back, the hair confusion match revived. After I had roughly followed the chain of command order again, we finally concluded that "the mess on my head" was not an issue. I believe the straw that broke the camel's back happened when one of the drummers quit but didn't inform the proper staff. He had been absent for multiple church services that I ended up playing in. Being told that I would not get anything for filling in for the drummer three weeks in a row, plus two funerals evolved into a heated debate.

If you have ever been involved in a smaller church congregation, then you will understand that confusion runs rapidly throughout the flock, mostly due to miscommunication—which is what I believe this ended up being. After being told that I would not get anything, I had a bit of diarrhea of the mouth, but I mainly wanted to plead my case to the minister that I just needed enough money to get back to school. I was again told no, so I took matters into my own hands by taking a few pieces of equipment from the older drum set at the church until I could receive some compensation to get to school. That compensation never came, but I did find myself receiving threats of charges being pressed and had a number of calls with many asking me to send the equipment back. This was completely out of my character, which amazed me even more that no one would ask why I took it in the first place. Had I been taught church politics of any other type of *proper* workplace behavior, then maybe there could've been a different outcome. I wasn't even being offered a portion of the payment due for my services rendered.

Around that time, the pay scale for religious musicians was near one hundred thirty dollars per service. My regular fill-in pay was one hundred dollars per event. If I were to give a home church half off, I was still owed four hundred dollars, but all I asked was sixty-five bucks. That was the cost of a greyhound ticket to Houston and a snack.

This was the winter break following my first full year of junior college. It was a whole new realm for me. I guess the stresses of being homeless while having to live off five to ten dollars a week for breakfast, lunch, and dinner on my own, as well as still attending a full-time schedule. I thought leaving home would take me away from such struggles, but boy, was I wrong in the matter? Some would say yes, but my mother had lost her job. My brother hustling was the only income source outside the money received from my father's child support, which helped her pay the bills. Anything I had left went to help my sister, who had gone off to school a few years prior. She didn't know how she was making ends meet. She was still dealing with the stresses of my dad, but my brother's top priority was taking care of his son, my nephew until that came to a halt when he was caught and given an extended jail sentence. I think by that time, everyone I knew was going hungry.

I did get a Pell Grant, which helped keep me in school. It also helped me pay for classes but not all of my books. There was no way we could afford a meal plan at our school, and there were months when Greg and I were trying to make ten bucks for food stretch for a week at a time.

I remember walking into the cafeteria one afternoon with a buck-fifty in my pocket. There were prepackaged sandwiches with lots of meat, burgers, pizza, munchies, and I thought about the six quarters I had. Even the soup was $1.95 and out of my league. The only things I could get were two tiny bags of Fritos and a can of Coke.

There weren't any dorm rooms available either, no room at the inn. So I echoed my earlier life, and Greg and I drifted around on a pretty regular basis. We stayed with a woman friend of his family for a semester, but she got into a new relationship, and out we went. At the beginning of the next semester we slept in the park and in Greg's car, neither of which was good for our backs.

Next, we were blessed to stay at Greg's uncle's place, but that went by fast too. I considered staying at my great aunt's, but two young men running in and out of her home did not seem like a good idea for an eighty-year-old lady. She was sweet, but she didn't need us barging in at all hours of the night.

We ran out of options, and we were back sleeping in Greg's car, and a day or two turned into weeks. We walked around hunched over with sore backs for a while. We used the campus recreational center for hygiene needs until we scored a spot with an ex-high school teammate who had some floor space. He and his friend smoked a lot, but they were super laid back.

We didn't have any beds, just the floor, but it was a step-up from sleeping in a car. Although there wasn't any hot water, we played dominoes and video games, and they never asked us for a dime. I thought our luck was changing, but then I found out my high school sweetheart was talking to another guy, then around the same time, one of my close family members was taken from us. This was the cousin that I had dedicated my locks to, but the old saying seemed to play on repeat as a whisper in my conscious, "When it rains, it pours, and it rained a lot that year."

Eventually, I landed a job at the local YMCA in their after-school tutoring program. I liked being a mentor, having some influence with the kids, and the money helped. It took a little pressure off the finances, but I was so busy! My GPA took a hit, but it meant Greg got a few bucks for gas, and I got to celebrate with the occasional luxury of Earl Campbell hotlink sausages to go with my *Ramen Noodles*.

I had a few ups and lots of downs but survived the year playing intramural football to stay in shape and getting at least one nice meal a week at the Baptist Student Ministry's Friday Night Pancake and Bacon get-together.

Those were good nights, and after we filled our bellies, Greg and I would spend the evening beating the pants off the BSM staff at spades and dominoes, which irked 'em a little, but it was fun. I also volunteered at church functions and Mission Arlington with the BSM staff for Christmas. It was a busy time with school and training and work, but it took my mind away from the negativity that pressed my way. Being flexible enough to get a job aided in the wishful thinking of better days to come. I had to give a little, since it did affect my grade point average, but I was positioning myself for the ultimate come up.

Naive Island

*"For me, winning isn't something that
happens suddenly on the field when
the whistle blows and the crowd roars.
Winning is something that builds
physically and mentally every day that
you train and every night that you
dream."*

-Emmitt Smith

My wrist and arm finally healed. I had to stop therapy because of it after the first two weeks. I felt I was ready after a year's time. I was anxious to see what would happen when football rolled around again. Actually, football might roll around, but it's a steamroller if you aren't ready, so I was really pushing myself. Still, I wasn't too keen on the idea of staying at the JuCo, since the program was in questionable shape, and I wasn't much impressed with the coaching situation. Soon, things changed. Not at this college, but elsewhere.

The University of Houston (UH) was not my first, second, or third choice for a college education or football. I was completely naive of the school's existence. It was completely off my radar, but one of my best friends, John, who initially went off to college in Louisiana, talked it up. He had left school the year before and convinced me to join him as he made his way closer to home.

John kept me encouraged and was excellent when offering solutions during our high school tenure. He pitched the idea that the UH campus was on the rise and how underrated was the football team. They were underdogs at the time, a nearly unrated school. He had me pumped about walking-on to the team and how he would be taking the field with me if I came out there. With their unheralded athletics program, Houston started to feel like the perfect place for me.

The rest of the nation joined me in sleeping in the presence of the University of Houston. I talked with my homie Greg who took the journey at the JuCo with me, and although Greg never walked on, I thought he might give it a shot at UH. As he sat by the car, he observed the program and was not feeling it. He mention that the reason he didn't try out at the JuCo was due to the coaches' lack of knowledge, and there was a lot of uncertainty about their football program. Yeah, I got that, but I hate that he couldn't build some level of *no fucks given* and just give it a shot.

I personally thought Greg didn't want to step out of his comfort zone. Walking on meant he'd be in some compromising situations, which he wasn't used to. It required a level of *flexibility* in the *walk-on mentality*, and he wasn't ready to adjust. Although we were both short in height as children, he was fast coming up in high school. His growth spurt got there a lot earlier than mine, and by our senior year, he was used to being a top-tier athlete on the team, one who didn't have to prove himself on a daily basis.

Our sole reason for attending a JuCo was to give us a chance to get noticed and earn a scholarship to a four-year school. Trying out left more chances for failure than success, and failure wasn't an anticipated option for Greg, so he disqualified himself before someone else could. I went through the test alone.

As for UH, Greg figured he'd be at a disadvantage trying to walk on without a scholarship and that he wouldn't get a fair opportunity. I thought maybe that was so, but that possibility wasn't going to stop me from trying. Trying out for UH was a big step-up from the JuCo level. Still, instead of seeing it as a roadblock, trying to walk on without a scholarship, I looked at UH as a positive opportunity and a new beginning for my college career. Seeing this as the challenge I needed, helped clear the brush as I prepared to enter by next island.

I told myself that I would have a place to stay, I would stay healthy as I walked on, and that not getting a meal plan was out of the question since I'd earn that too. I figured I'd have no more struggles and heartache. I was putting in the work and the mental preparation to handle any crisis. I was sure the result would be a more focused college life, ensuring I could graduate. But again, I was naive.

Setback Island

"Instead of trying to build a brick wall,
lay a brick every day. Eventually, you'll
look up, and you'll have a brick wall."

-Nipsey Hussle

My buddy, John, went to college with the party-first, homework-later mentality, which quickly got him shipped back to Texas. It's very common with first-year students. There's a lot of freedom awarded to you on campus, which is cool, only if you balance your work with your play. If you can't, it's a disaster. Your classes become impossible to attend on time, your tests are your enemies, and your report cards expose the fun you had and the learning you missed. One too many parties did it for John. He hoped UH would be different.

Even though I didn't want to go to Houston, being on the campus of a university in the Spring of 2009 gave me a sense of pride. It was like, yes, my past was shit, but this next step will be better; It had to be.

If you've never made it down to Houston, it's about 250 miles south-east of Texas's middle, right on the Gulf of Mexico. It's got more people than any other city in the state, and the summers are brutal, long, hot, and humid. You get temperatures over 90 degrees every day, 100 degrees sometimes.

Now that might not sound bad, but let's face it, the city is on the coast. Houston has subtropical humidity, a sweet way of saying it's sweltering unless you were born on the sun. Summer mornings average 90% humidity. It was crazy for me, like walking into a steam room. THAT humidity is like no other. Cold, hot, windy, or even a perfect 70-degree overcast brought the *meat sweats*. In my first week, I thought I wouldn't make it. Just walking outside made me sweat buckets, but there I was, and I made up my mind to stay and get my degree.

I was there, signed up, and ready to go, but then there were some financial aid issues. The paperwork never seems to go through the first time, and the response and your loans never seem to come back on time. When they did, they weren't right, which meant I would be without housing. I started thinking, *man, some things never change*, and again, I was right back to sleeping on the floor in John's dorm. It was no "Sealy, Posture-Pedic morning" for me. Man, my back ached.

I hadn't gotten my Associate of Arts Degree at the JuCo, and I found out that I wasn't eligible to play ball at UH that year because of it, which cost me the opportunity to be a walk-on athlete or chance to earn a scholarship. I was a long way from Mansfield with another setback and started feeling homesick with the residue of *Homeless Island* hanging over my head.

My student loan money came late, as I later figured to be a norm, and standing in line to get my books for the semester was very stressful. I managed to pay for all of my books but one out of all of my classes. Lectures were way more extensive than the ones at the JuCo, but my professors were reasonable people and kept my interest well enough for me to get solid grades, all A's and B's on the first round of testing.

The University of Houston is a big school, with more than 40,000 students, so I made plenty of friends. I had study groups where we met regularly to hash-out our homework assignments and socialized on a more personal basis. It was getting nice; I started to feel accepted, and I liked it.

At one point, I met someone whose company I enjoyed, and we hung at the Student Center Satellite between classes regularly, where we had meal plans. Although I was in love with my high school sweetheart, I still got involved with this woman and cheated. That part wasn't adversity; it was stupidity, but none the less, another point for *Setback Island*. Both of the ladies deserved better. Jas and I quickly moved on, but the lingering issues it presented to my relationship back home were long-lasting.

Houston was the first place I felt that I was too far from home, and in the middle of my first semester, I was drifting around, trying to get my bearings. My friend John and I grew apart since we didn't see each other often, and then my grandmother passed away.

It's always devastating to lose a loved one. My grandmother was a big part of our family, and going home for the funeral put things in perspective for me. It also had a profound effect on my father. As tough as his drug addiction might have been, losing his mother hit him harder than any pipe he ever had. He was a man, a grown man, but he looked lost for a while. That time could have been his worst ever and an almost reasonable one for him to binge on whatever he thought would soothe him.

To his credit, there were changes for the better afterward, and he made a real effort to get himself together. I did the same thing at college.

I made sure I got to my classes on time, and I designed a training program to stay in shape for football. *Setback Island* wouldn't keep me down. By that time, there wasn't anything that would stop me from getting my degree, and I made sure it was the same as becoming a Cougar and playing football for the University of Houston.

Preparation Island

"I hated every minute of training, but I said, 'Don't quit. Suffer now and live the rest of your life as a champion.'"
-Muhammad Ali

When you're a kid, going to college seems a lot like just another four years of high school. No problem, right? And then, bam, you get introduced to the real world. Like many students, my high school years were tough enough, but college makes you knuckle down and get serious. If you skimp on preparation, things breeze past you and you realize you're gone with the wind before you know what happened.

I thought I was ready when my second semester at UH started. I got to my classes, set up a workout regime, and tempered my weekends by resisting the urge to party and loosen up with friends. I did that by deciding what was essential and prioritizing my schedule, classes, and studies. Doing that took a lot of discipline, especially since I knew I had another semester before trying to walk on to the football team.

Again, I started in the spring at UH, and the NCAA required students participating in sports had to have a year of residency before playing if you've not earned a bachelor's degree or failed to earn an Associate of Arts degree at the JuCo.

Since then, they have made minor changes to the rule, but it was weird since a football coach can transfer to another college and go to work immediately. Student-athletes are held to a different standard, and there are many bizarre and byzantine rules you have to follow.

The other problem I started to stress over was what my major should be. I'd spent so much time getting ready to play football that I hadn't thought much about what my life's work might be. Maybe it was because it's so hard to make a college football squad, and that was where my mind was a lot of the time. Perhaps I had been on *Naive Island* longer than I thought, and now *Preparation Island* was exposed.

According to the NCAA, there are about 1 million high schoolers who play football. But less than 7% of those student-athletes who were good enough to make their high school teams have the talent to make a college football team. That percentage includes division three and division two schools. I had a friend, London, that went right to a division three school to play ball. He was a D1 player in my book, and the competition isn't as tough on the D3 level. There are no full-ride scholarships, and the schools are smaller, more like a JuCo. He was someone I considered a better athlete than me, and there I was trying to make it at a top-tier, division one school with 40,000 students. What was I thinking?

The semester started better since I wasn't sleeping on someone's floor. My back didn't hurt as much, and I felt well-rested. I'd managed to get in a dorm room with a cool roommate, and he was on the football team. We were way up high on the tenth floor with a hell of a view but having him there connected to the football program helped my mental outlook. He had a lot of insights for me.

With student loans, I finally had enough money for all my classes and books and a UH meal plan, which I supplemented with *Ramen Noodles* when my stomach pleaded for more after the workouts had sapped my strength. By that time, I was 5'10 and just over 200 pounds. I tested my strength and speed against opponents in intramural football and kept my plan alive for becoming a Cougar.

James, my roommate, encouraged me to keep training. He said, "Dude, you're as fast as anybody in our secondary; you could be playing safety for us right now." That helped immensely, especially as I trained in the weight room alone. That was a piece of well-timed encouragement since that weight room was no joke.

Training is as mentally taxing as it is physically. You've got to have a plan, and you've got to stick with it. It's easy to stay in bed in the morning at college, and I fought with that desire every day, but I had one other thing on my mind, and that was the desire to be the first one in my family to earn their college degree. My folks were encouraging me, and that was a blessing and a burden because I didn't want to let anyone down, but your friends and family can only do so much. So, I fought the desire to give up and became even more disciplined.

I hit the weights every day, knowing that nobody ever drowned in their sweat, but I tried. Man, I tried. I got a work-study job between books and study and classes through the University Career Services program at UH. The career center works with students and alumni in job search and career plans. They helped me with getting work, which helped me choose a major.

As much as I loved football and working out to reach that football goal, I had the idea that I might also be pretty good as a coach. With those things in mind, I began leaning toward getting a Bachelor of Science degree in Kinesiology. That would mean I'd be doing lifelong learning, thinking, and action training while studying the biomechanical, physiological, and sociological perspectives that interact with physical activity from the human body's cells and stretching into humankind and society. I figured that would keep me healthy, happy, and very busy.

That semester I won a Cougar Card Scholarship and started playing the drums again. I was both surprised and angry with hopping back on the drum throne at first because I was just horrible, but I knew it was because I hadn't been playing and had those genuine leather veins to stretch out from the broken wrist. It had been a long time since I picked up the sticks, and my muscle memory and rhythm were shot.

I sat ruminating about my drum playing for a while but convinced myself it was just the lack of practice. Instead of being disappointed, I turned the frustration around and used it as motivation to keep doing my football workouts and not falling behind in my weight training. I didn't want the last five years of hard work to be for nothing.

My spirit was intact, but I was so busy that my relationship with the most important person in my life was falling apart. We were too far apart, physically and spiritually, at the time. We weren't connecting, and I was driving all my thoughts and time into college and training. That's a bad combination for any couple. Fortunately, she's amazing and understanding. She cut me a lot of slack. While I was busy with football and school, Jas went to college to become a nurse. She was patient and understanding through all of this, and she always wanted what was best for me and lend a helping hand when she could. She allowed me to be me—even when the going was rough—which is one of the many reasons she earned first dibs whenever we said, "I do," years later.

The same issues cropped up with my family and friends. I was the bad guy for not keeping up with them, but I only had 24-hours each day, like everyone else, and finding time for telephone talks and drives home was impossible. Even if the comfort of home and my loved ones were just what I needed sometimes, I was unable to please everyone. Sometimes, this was due to the amount of time given in a single day and other times, due to the lack of preparation. Even God took multiple days to complete his vision. Who am I to get all mine done in one?

Residual Island

"Six in one hand, half a dozen in the other."

-Florence Douglas, Mother

We all have opportunities, and we weigh them out as best we can to make the choices that send us in one direction or another; pick one, or maybe the other. By my second year at UH, I was confident I was in the right place. My mother and dad were doing better together, and Jas and I were trying. I could only imagine that my mother, who I hadn't talked to for a while, was stressed out, thanks to my dad. I never did find out whether my dad was getting better with his recovery, though it was never something they talked about with me. I was sure that my mother is doing a lot better with my dad now, likely with a stable place to live. My focus was now on making the Cougar football team.

Throwing a pass or running for a touchdown looks easy on TV because the athletes are so good. They are in prime shape, mainly because they are talented and have been playing competitively for years. It's fun to watch.

Sure, they have talent, but nature didn't make Michael Jordan perfect for throwing down dunks or sinking 30-footers any more than Tiger Woods, who woke up one morning able to drive the ball 300-yards. It's just the opposite.

Woods was an early starter. His father, former college baseball player Earl Woods, introduced him to golf. He was a child prodigy, but he couldn't have been one if he didn't start getting groomed at two. His dad was fanatical about him playing golf. Woods got lessons, worked his tail off, and once he was in college, he was weight training, which almost no other golfers were doing, putting that extra distance on his drives.

Anyone can play ball in the street, but not many people can make a college or professional team in their chosen sport. It's a full-time job, especially if you get a full-ride scholarship. A scholarship player's involvement and their performance on the field serve as payment for their education. Colleges make nearly one billion dollars from their sports pro-grams, and football is the biggest cash cow of them all.

And then, there are the walk-on players. They are a different breed. Don't get me wrong, some are trash, but some have talent and a big chip on their shoulders, making them tough and mean. In the same process, the tough and mean ones can also get exposed when facing someone just as tough and mean, making them so defensive that they lose sight of their original goal and objectives. They know that somehow, they slipped through the cracks on their way through high school and didn't get noticed. Though they still show up at a college and do the work, and against all the odds, they make the team. It's rare, but it happens, thank goodness, so I had some slim hope to cling to.

I talked early to walk-on coordinator Joe Alcos-er, and he gave me the rundown on how I might be able to try out and make the team. My chances didn't look good, but after several years of physical training and mental preparation, I was more confident than he was. Even though the smirk on Joe's face read as me being one out of one hundred athletes singing the same tune, I was determined to show him and whoever else that I was that dude.

Having to put yourself out there against the odds is scary, but sometimes you've got to roll the dice and have some faith. I was a church boy, after all.

I'll get into prep, drills, training, and such in a second, but I'll cut the story short by just saying that it was my time to shine. Fortunately, I was ready and had a great series of tryouts. Unlike at junior college, UH had a more high-paced system, and I mastered every drill during the station sequence. This structure seemed familiar to the exercise groups that I had done back in middle school. The coach named it 'county fair.' I wasn't certain where the title stemmed from, given there was much amusing about them, but it was one of the hardest things I had done in my life at that point.

This go-round, I was better prepared. It wasn't easy, but I had been battle-tested in drill, skills, and knowledge of the game by a student turned Master Carlos Francis. He was my guide to how college football would be for me. At this point, I didn't care how hard the tryouts were anyways. They were going to have to drag me off the Carl Lewis Field passed out from exhaustion. There were more guys on the practice fields than I'd ever seen at one time to ball out, but I couldn't care less. That morning, I was full steam ahead, and nobody was going to take my moment.

The coaches moved guys through drills; speed turns, seat rolls, sprints, catching passes, hitting, blocking, tackling, and then off; some guys would go to other places on the practice facility, or a coach would come by and send you home.

Like that, I tried out for strong defensive safety and free safety, and once again, there was a hell of a lot more guys trying out than there were spots on the roster. Still, I liked the safety position, and it was mine for the taking. A safety is kind of what it sounds like: the team's last line of defense to keep a player from scoring. As a strong safety, you're in tune with the other teams running in-game and work as a moving linebacker who's also fast enough to cover receivers.

As a free safety, you have to be smart enough and confident enough to lay back a little and survey the offensive structure and see what develops, then attack where the ball goes. I loved the position because you're in on every play, at least mentally, and that's how I made the team a strong/ free safety. Yes, I finally made the freaking squad.

I was a little afraid to be excited. The way I was, a celebration wasn't in the cards for me. I was worried that I would relax too much and miss out on the next step in earning a scholarship. Added, I wasn't a soar winner. I didn't want to rub it in for those who had not yet reach that pentacle. My dudes were not there to share my good news with. I was excited about it, but this was a small accomplishment that wasn't to be celebrated anyways. The perfectionist in me wouldn't allow me to dwell on what I thought was a low-level accomplishment. I was ready to play wherever there was an opening, whatever got me on the field for the scout team, whether it was as a safety, a cornerback, or even a linebacker at this point.

Practices were as strenuous as anything I could have ever imagined. Making the team was tough enough, but drawing playing time was going to be more challenging. Did I mention that it's hot and humid in Houston? Well, of course. But try doing drills with shoulder pads, knee pads, thigh pads, hip pads, plus a helmet keeping all that heat on your head. It isn't a breeze.

During the second week of spring practice, I was surprised when one of the coaches came over and said, "TD, head over to the offensive coordinator and talk to him." I wasn't sure what was up, but I did it.

The coach wanted me for the offense as a running back. I didn't care to ask why. I had no issue with it since I felt at home in the backfield from my childhood periods, but I was way behind the other backs after two-weeks of practice. I didn't know the playbook, and I got thrown straight into the inside hole group, big blocks, multiple times. Inside hole drill is the period of practice that is normally the most upbeat due to the high collisions. It's sometimes the only period that the first-team offense would be in full contact with the first-team defense just outside the goal line. This is the drill that you have to let your nuts hang to and was known to separate the men from the boys. Either you scored, or you were stopped.

Coach McKinney told one of the vets, Andre, to show me what to do. "Yo, TD, first make sure to line up on the inside foot of the tackle. Then it's you and the D-end. Attack him inside out. Alright, Coach, he's ready."

"You in next play," says Coach. Crawford Jones yells his cadence, "go hit!" And I take off' balls to the wall' and smack! I and the DE collide. Everyone standing around yelled "woo!" as if the collision summoned the great Rick Flair in them all. Coach McKinney runs up, slaps my shoulder pads with excitement, pulls me back to the backfield, and says, "Okay! Okay! Do it again." And... Smack! Smack! Smack! These actions repeated over and over. I got one or two plays off, then back at it again with the hard-hitting. Then, I was finally rewarded with a handoff.

The first day on the job was a proper welcome to college football moment.

As we wrapped up the drill and I was finally able to breathe, Marcell Bates dapped me up then complimented me, saying, "Man, that was you over there? You had it sounding like gunshots."

The transition worked out fantastically, and I had a chance to carry the ball several times in practice. When our first scrimmage game rolled around,

I knew a few plays and felt a little comfortable with the offensive scheme. I got a few carries, and I was the only running back to score in the game. I was feeling good.

A lot had changed in my life since playing drums and playing ball, and since missing football in JUCO to changing positions at UH. You've got to be willing to adjust in football and life. There's nothing wrong with modifying your plans and moving in a new direction by accepting feedback. Know yourself and be true to yourself, and you will find that path you need to take.

When you're in that frame of mind, you'll accept that the more you know, the more you realize you don't know shit. The change will happen, life is hard, and adversity will present itself at every turn. Your flexibility determines how quickly you can pivot when something goes wrong.

Still, football is a tough game, and Coach Sumlin might not have been too happy with how the team looked at the end of that scrimmage. I remember him sounding angry and saying, "Coach Phillips, go ahead."

What Coach Phillips said confirmed my thoughts. "Hey fellas, we didn't handle business today. I saw sloppy routes, loafs, and defense came to play with a chip on their shoulder. We didn't go on offense."

"That's right," said Sumlin. "You guys better listen up!"

"Yup," said Phillips. "You get better, or you get worse. You can't stay the same and expect to win any games. Today was a piss poor job, fellas. We didn't get better, and I don't even know his name, but number 45 was the only one that came to play on offense. We're supposed to be 'The Show.' Now, we gon' have to figure out how to get back to where we should be, fellas."

It didn't register at first since I started with jersey number 4 but was switched to 45 with the position reassignment. A few of the fellas began to peek back at me with a head nod of excitement that sent chills through my arms. I was pretty ecstatic, but I kept a poker face. Plus, the coaches weren't done chewing us out.

"Alright, thanks, coach," said Sumlin. "Defense, you guys didn't do a bad job today. You still got a lot you need to clean up, though. A couple of you got a little self-righteous out there. We are out here to compete, but don't get it twisted. Don't try to be THE man; just be A man, and the system will take care of everything else."

"Offense," he continued, "we didn't get anywhere close to the number of plays we were supposed to run today. It's like we forgot how to play fast. As the coach said, we didn't show that we were ready to play a game today, but that's okay. Next week, we're going to pick up the tempo, so don't get left behind. Make sure you play fast but not in a hurry. Alright, Case (quarterback Case Keenum), wrap us up."

That wasn't an unwarranted speech, the coaches wanted us to do better, to work more as a team, and I think everyone on the squad wished the same thing, so we keep working harder as a team.

Afterward, I found out that the walk-ons didn't get to eat with the other team players, those on scholarship. It sounds crazy, and you'd think the coaches and administrators would want the players together as a team, but that's not the way it was. Walk-ons had to pay for their meals, so lucky for me, I had a meal plan and my packs of crumbly, Japanese noodles.

I had a good rapport with a few coaches, who said they felt that I was the top walk-on in the system. I hoped that meant I'd get a full-ride someday. But that's something else that's weird about NCAA football. When you're a walk-on, they don't say, "Wow, you're a great player," and give you a scholarship. No. They use you up all year, and then at the end of the season, the standout walk-ons and senior walk-ons may have a shot at scholarships, and this wasn't a guarantee.

That's not entirely on the coaches, though. That's straight from the NCAA because a team only gets so many scholarships per year, and they use them up on their previously scouted incoming freshmen players. I knew what I was getting myself into, so I couldn't complain, but it sucked, nonetheless.

Facing that was a harsh lesson, but if I'd learned anything in my life, it was to be flexible.

Resilient & Wakeup Island

"The thing you can't measure is someone's heart, someone's desire. You can measure a 40, his vertical, his bench press, and that might let you know things like, yeah, he can jump high, but desire, his dedication, his determination, that's something you can't measure."

- Shannon Sharpe

I was still learning the team's offensive plays in our first month of practice, and I got a little help from a couple of the other running backs. There's a lot of competition between the players. Everyone wants to make the team and get playing time, so all guys are grinding but don't want to share much information.

Grudgingly, they gave a little, and I stretched those lessons out as much as I could.

I had to try and get along with those guys, the good and the bad, and work with the coaches, which was hard because I'd always had some issues with older guys that I felt didn't care about me going back to my mother's dating days. I wouldn't say I liked the power-trip authority over me, but once you recognize the knowledge being offered, you've got to buy-in.

During that time, I learned that you had to be careful of whom you talked to. A fellow RB and I shared concerns about the possibility of us not getting playing time. We talked about how our attributes sized up to the scholarship players. Word gets around fast on a sports team. Sometimes, it's harmless; sometimes, it ain't. Footballs aren't round, so you can't predict how they'll bounce, and practice is like that too.

I was pumped after our first scrimmage: Rockin' and rollin'. Then the second scrimmage comes around a week later, and I don't get a single carry. Didn't run the ball once.

I spent a lot of time trying to figure that out. You can't go whine to the coaches and cry about not getting playing time as a walk-on, not if you expect to get any in the future, but it pissed me off. So, what was it? Did a coach think I was slacking in practice?

Did I make an enemy? Did I do too much? Did I not do enough? Who knows?

All I knew at the moment was that a scholarship player was getting moved to run back when the summer started, and that meant less action for the walk-ons. The lack of playing time as an RB carried over to the summer workouts. Maybe that put me too far down the depth chart, but I chose to do my best when given the opportunity. The player hierarchy is a funny thing.

Sometimes, players who are walk-ons get the shit-end of the stick. I hate to put it that way, but it's true. Sometimes the better players don't play. You see, the university doesn't have any money invested in walk-ons, but someone's reputation is riding on the scholarships. It's not the player's fault, kind of, and coaches want to win. Unless you're a monster talent like LaDainian Tomlinson or Todd Gurley, it's easy to get buried.

Another issue was when the team would use players as tackling dummies for the starting squad. Who do you think the starting defensive team played against in practice most of the time? Well, it ain't the starting offensive team. You play against the "C" squad, which comprises a lot of walk-ons and some scholarship players. A lot of the walk-on guys played with that chip on their shoulder. This gets easier as you are consistently overlooked. You must create your opportunities to be seen.

As a running back, you might carry the ball through a hole in the line for a nice gain before the defense would finally get to thud you up. Then the coach gets sensitive because the defense can't stop the backup's backup and decides to reload the play for another shot of success. You get the ball, hit the line, and now you get crushed. Not because the defense is so good but solely because we just ran the same freaking play, and they knew what was coming. Sometimes, they would even put a little extra on the point of contact whenever they're pissed, or you're making them look bad, and the coach chews them out.

Is that unfair? Yep. But when you get HIT with unfairness, it can have a profound IMPACT on you. Situational unfairness has a huge bearing on how you view yourself and others. Anybody can do well in a comfortable situation. To be great, you must make yourself comfortable with being uncomfortable, which is why I took pride in making the defense look bad on the reloaded plays also.

Following my first full spring of football at a university, I went into the summer workouts with a lot of hunger and a little anger used to prove myself.

Strength and Conditioning Coach Jackson's program used to whoop my ass. I can still hear him to this day: "Let's go, fellas! You know what it is. It's live at 5:45 am!"

I wasn't a morning person, so waking up at 4:30 every day was for the birds. Most mornings, I was so nervous about missing my alarm that I would wake up rushing to the Alumni athletic building, forgetting to check the clock. One time, I was halfway there before realizing that I had a whole hour of extra time that I could have still been asleep. I was pissed, but I went ahead to the complex to take my routine wake-up shower. The daily workouts were tough enough, and I'd rather be too early than too late. The punishment was thirty minutes on the *Stairmaster*; then, you had to complete the workout of the day. I had difficulty completing the workout itself, so I wasn't about that life with being late.

I was tired every day, giving 100% in the weight room, on the field, doing community services at kid's camps, and serving food to the homeless when I was on the brink of starvation with the cafeteria being closed on campus. It was summer, and when you're in school, you look forward to being off. You get to sleep in, but not now. After workouts, class, film study, routes, and everything else. When I got back to the dorm at night, I was ready to crash.

I was living on campus in the Towers dormitory on the 10th floor. Workouts ended around 6:30 am, and soon after, I had a two-hour class at 8:30 am. I would shower, have a little breakfast, meet up with another class at 11 am, then lunch. I did homework afterward and had a self-film study at 2 pm for football. We had route running and 7on7 practice at 5:30 pm. Then, when I had the energy, I would complete an additional film session late in the evening after dinner, sometimes until 1 a.m., attempting to perfect the complex offensive system.

Thinking back on it now gets my blood pumping. Though Man, I hate that I loved it so much cause I freaking loved it.

My summer meals were the same nearly every day: microwave eggs for breakfast; sandwiches, chips, and two oranges for lunch, then Ramen noodles for dinner. I filled my water jug from the water fountain down the hall. It seemed like I wasn't far from home, where I used to get water from the vacant building's faucet, minus the dingy tinted Houston water that I had no choice but to drink.

Weight training was four days a week, and by mid-summer, I was the strongest and fastest I've ever been. I could rep 405 pounds on the bench press and squat 500 pounds. That's like having three people upon your shoulders and squatting down as low as you can go and then standing up straight.

The years of sports and hard knocks leading up to playing football at UH taught me to be prepared. I committed to taking on the challenges that life presented and was willing to put in the time and effort it took to improve every situation.

I mentally prepared so I could take advantage of opportunities as they appeared. I had a plan, and while it took flexibility and optimism to get where I was going, I constantly strategized and built towards the future. When you do that, others that see your passion will be there to pick you up when you need it most. Life, like football, is a team sport.

I worked hard; held nothing back. I worked my tail off for the opportunity to climb up the depth chart and earn some real game time. I also looked forward to earning one

One-Shot Island

"It doesn't cost you nothing to speak."
                                    -Eugene Wilson

Before the football season started, I was still happy about being on the team. I'd made it as a walk-on, but I started seriously thinking about getting that scholarship. I work so hard for it, but if I could get it, it meant meals with the team and no need for a campus meal plan. No more hungry nights, no more noodle soup, no more struggles to pay for classes or books, but there's always a catch.

Scholarships don't guarantee you a ride for all four years or two if you transfer in from a JuCo. What they don't tell you is that when you commit to a scholarship, you agree to a one-year renewable contract. People sign-up, and then they find out that you can be just as disposable as the player that just walked-on. I have even heard of coaches pulling

95

scholarships prior to the student-athletes comple-
tion of their senior graduation.

It sounds harsh, but that's only because it is!
Your scholarship can go bye-bye if you get into
trouble on the field and off the field. Sometimes, a
new coach wants to mold his image into the team,
and out you go. Even if you're physically still there,
you're treated like just another body for scout and
special teams. Bad grades also disqualify you from
eligibility, so if your act isn't right, coaches are quick
to dump you. If you got the goods, then you're safe
for the most part.

Don't get me wrong, I still loved football and
wanted a scholarship. You don't know if you haven't lived it, and many people don't talk about it.
Towards the end of summer workouts, I started to
feel like my grind was going unnoticed, and then
Strength and Conditioning Coach Jackson pulled
me aside early on and said, "I see you working your
ass off every day. You deserve a shot, and I spoke up
for you. Don't mess it up."

I didn't even realize it when he said it, but that
put a lot of pressure on me. Still, those words helped
to solidify my spot for the team's 105-man camp
before the beginning of the fall season. Scholarship
players got first dibs off the top, but the elite walk-
on's earned it. Coach's words of encouragement
went a long way for my mental stability through the
final weeks of workouts. Getting into camp was big.

Camp days included breakfast, meetings, weight room workouts, and walkthroughs. Then we had brunch, more meetings to discuss plays and player assignments, and more walkthrough drills (no pads, not hitting), but practice came later each day. Like I said before, it's like a full-time job.

There was a little fun, like the talent – no talent show. I had grown my hair and had long twisted locks, but one of my peers was in the beginning stages of his, so the vets gave him the bit 'I am not my hair-India Arie' to sing. The team was rolling. It was all in good fun.

I wasn't laughing much the next day because my teammates left me asleep, and I was late for workouts. I got a 30-minute Stairmaster routine as a penalty; then, I still had to complete the assigned workout for the morning. With the lack of reps through summer drills, I was still a little behind on the offensive program. Confusion was still running rampant about my position on the depth chart, but Receiver Coach Phillips pulled me to the side and explained how the system worked. That's what good coaches do, they work with you instead of against you, and it helped. Long story short, I don't suck, and "it's a business."

Finally, a better understanding of the politics of the program. I kept working as hard as humanly possible. So hard that I put my body through everything it could handle every week. So hard that I made myself throw up during every Friday workout; those Friday sled days were unforgettable.

We had what looked like an excellent team. We had a strong quarterback, Case Keenum, who's playing in the NFL today. At running back, Michael Hayes, who joined the team, was from Texas JuCo Blinn College and a terrific player.

That was great for the team, and I was happy, but it was tough for me because we also had Bryce Beall, a super-strong back who ended his career at Houston as the third all-time leading rusher in Cougar history. We had Charles Sims; he was the truth and later played in the NFL. There was a lot of talent. I don't have enough ink to go into all of the speed and talent we had as wide receivers. We had a chance to be a great team.

I wish I could say the year ended well, but Keenum tore his ACL (anterior cruciate ligament) in our third game against UCLA, and we struggled to a 5-7 record. It sucked for me too. With all those star running backs in front of me, I worked for playing time, and then like Keenum, I ruptured my ACL too. I knew I would recover, but I was numb to the fact that that injury may have cost me my chance at earning my scholarship. I was pissed, sad, depressed, you name it. I tried thinking optimistically as Coach said that I was ok but needed to give my knee time to heal.

There isn't much you can do to speed up recovery from an ACL surgery. You just limp along the best you can until the doctors tell you it's time to start physical therapy, also known as torture therapy. Then, it's anywhere from two to six months before you feel like a halfway regular person and up to nine months before you can get back to playing ball. I already told you about therapy for my wrist, but it was nothing compared to trying to come back from an ACL. It was an SOB.

Because an ACL tear is so monumental to the body, mostly occurring during sports that involve sudden stops or changes in direction, I didn't have the range of motion necessary to join the team in 2010. Still, I kept going to therapy, classes, and like Keenum, I missed the whole year. Another roadblock.

On another note, college is tough on everyone, including one of my suitemates. The guy was wound-up too tight, a basket case after a tough year, and then he tried to harm himself in his room, inside our dorm. He'd made a call-out earlier by phone to a family member, and then late that night, when the rest of us were asleep, the cavalry came charging in. The door was locked, so they kicked it in. Scared the hell out of us all.

He and I were cool. We would kick it from time to time until we had a disagreement due to someone walking out on their tab during a late-night food run. As we were on the brink of a brawl, I slowly began to revisit my goals for earning that scholarship and, more importantly, the promise I had made to my mother. I had a couple of run-ins with guys who were just not having good luck that I had grown patient enough, not just to react ignorantly.

My initial feelings about the situation were that I had made cowardly moves. Not too long after, I had a conversation with my cousin, JoJo, in the state prison about me feeling soft for not going for the blows.

He replied, "Man, scratch all that we use to tell y'all. Doing that stupid stuff is what helped to lead me here. You did right." Weirdly, this was more of a burden lifted off my shoulders than I understood had even existed.

In the close altercations that I walked away from, there may have been two that I still wonder if I made the right decision. I guess they had more issues than I could understand at that point but had we fought in those moments, there's no telling if this book would have even been written.

Fortunately for the roommate, he lived through both attempts of an altercation with me and inflicting harm on himself. As I said, college is tough on everyone, and we were all just kids. Sometimes, we don't realize what seems impossible; those roadblocks in front of us, the unimaginable adversity, can be overcome with practice, planning, and the faith that often eludes us.

Transition Island

"It is more difficult to stay on top than to get there."

– Mia Hamm

ootball consumed me for years, and then I was back at ground zero, unable to play. I missed the entire 2010 season and spent most of it trying to recover from my injury. When you're recovering as a walk-on, the road looks like one of those old Twilight Zone TV shows where the road keeps getting longer and longer– completely straight – and no end in sight. The difference between scholarship and a walk-on post-injury is when you finally get healed, the road you thought was ending ain't ending at all for the walk-on. You're basically back to the resilient island, working your way to the one-shot island all over again.

When I made the team as a walk-on, I moved my mental goalposts by buying into the system, hoping to get a scholarship. I worked as hard as I could, resulting in a lot of newcomers being convinced that I was indeed a scholarship athlete. It's those conversations that push me to continue with that walk-on mentality. That was a high level of respect to be given, and it was well deserved.

Many of us were just as good if not better than the scholarship players; we just took a more challenging, windier road to master the system to get in the game.

According to my coaches, my ability, attitude, and commitment made me stand out as an elite athlete. It was an accomplishment in itself, being recognized by coaches and other great athletes for my work. It was my way of leading with actions.

I remember what Coach Tony Levine said about me, "He's quick, an extremely hard worker, a perfectionist," which meant a lot to me.

Quarterback Crawford Jones was a little more colorful when he told me, "You're a fucking good athlete, and there was nothing you couldn't do, straight-line fast, strong, and complete in all areas needed."

Missing the 2010 season with the ACL tear gave me a feeling that seemed like the end of my scholarship dream, but I still wanted to play, and it was worth the pain for gain. I did make the 2011 team even though the team doctor wouldn't clear me to play on Saturdays. 2012 quickly approached.

By then, Case Keenum was gone, but the starting running back, Charles Sims, was still there.

I listened to everything my coaches said, never gave up, or refused to do anything. Our lineup was just another roadblock, adversity to be beaten. Everyone had hard times, I figured. It's how you manage those opportunities that determine the measurement of the man. Like QB, Coach Kliff Kingsbury would say, "Instead of bitching and complaining, make a play."

In the 2011 season, there were coaching changes that severely impacted the coming year. To start with, just before our bowl game, our Head Coach, Kevin Sumlin, told the team on December 10th that he was leaving after the team's almost undefeated season, with the upset loss to the University of Southern Mississippi, to take the Head Coach job at Texas A&M, effective immediately. It was just a few weeks before we were going to play in the Ticket City Bowl. Hence, the Athletic Department promoted our special team's coordinator, Tony Levine, to the Head Coach spot.

Coach told me later, "TD, it happened so fast. I slept in the office for the next ten nights as the interim coach before they gave me the Head Coach job."

That tells you how dedicated he was, trying to get the team ready for our bowl game. I've got a lot of respect for the man.

After our bowl game, Levine brought in Travis Bush in 2012 to be the running backs coach, so I worked with him a bit. After our loss in the first game of the season to the newly D1 promoted Texas State football squad, we lost our offensive coordinator, Mike Nesbitt. That left us with a big hole in the coaching core, so Coach Levine promoted Bush to our offensive coordinator, which was a huge jump in responsibility for him but us RBs were kind of left stranded. Change happens fast at the collegiate level, and I knew that very well when I got thrown back into the special teams' role.

In 2012, I was permanently placed on special teams. Special teams are what units on the team are called when the ball is being kicked around. Like punt kickoff and field goal, except I was too light in the pants for the field goal. It was a quick change and somewhat disappointing, but I was playing, and I just wanted to help the team. We needed it since things weren't going anything like they were the year before.

I was content with my position to help the team, but I will say that the competitor in me did feel that I could help the team better with the ball in my hands.

We were not prepared for the 2012 season, and we came up a little short of a bowl game that year.

We lost good players, good coaches and only managed to win five games that year after being nearly undefeated the year before. It was a huge letdown, but only one team can win each game.

I give the coaches a lot of credit since they worked as hard, if not harder, than the players. And, I learned about what I like to call "Perfect Practice." The coaches would manage practice in such a way to put us in game-like situations. The goal was to prepare each person so that there were no surprises on the field. You'd know what the obstacles were before you saw them on the field in a real game, and it was evident when done efficiently and inefficiently.

I've used that coaching style in my after-college life when training athletes. It's a good motivator and a great coaching aid to prepare players. Some players are prone to overthinking things, and some aren't sure what to do or think. You are learning how to adapt to whatever is thrown your way. That preparation is important in life, whether you are getting ready for a test, a date, an interview, or whatever. Not being prepared and learning corrective ways to handle situations will result in you or your team holding that "L."

Walk-On Island

*"Start by doing what's necessary; then
do what's possible, and suddenly you are
doing the impossible."*

-Francis of Assisi

Walk-on Island was our spot. A place in the
University of Houston locker room for the underappreciated. The athletes who were successful during
the county fair like tryout still understood that every
day was a test. It was a sanctuary within a sanctuary,
where we ran things. Scholarship players knew it
was our quarter, our domain. If a scholarship player
ever so much as poked their head into the walk-on
players' area, we grabbed them and tossed 'em back
out in a heartbeat. There were a few playful tussles,
but the locker room did respect our position. A selected few were allowed to mingle amongst the exclusive.

It was an essential part of us. We might have been one team, but there were segments: defense and offensive linemen in a pod; running backs, linebackers, wide receivers, and defensive backs grouped in another area; the quarterbacks and kickers lockers were near the star athletes on the team, and the last was all the walk-ons stuffed in our area. It was a little cliquish, but the walk-ons were a different breed. Our situation was different. We had all the positions in our area, and sometimes we had to share a locker with another player. We were like enlisted men in the military. The officers had it made; their quarters and the officer's mess were plush. The enlisted men worked every day. They carried the officers into battle.

On the football field and off, the scholarship guys had rights. The walk-ons couldn't earn without that piece of paper; that signed document that said they could stay after practice and have dinner together while we had to shower and leave quickly to the campus cafeteria.

Some carried an appreciated swagger with their scholarship. I call it the "scholo walk." This showed that even when that player had a horrible game or practice, he could be upset that he had just purchased that new fit with that stipend. And where there's good bad isn't too far behind with the two or three arrogant athletes that had to keep reminding you with their first world problems like; why do they keep feeding us steak and lobster; or man, I'm only going to be able to get one pair of Jordan's cause I got to buy these new rims with my stipend this month. I was being funny with the steak and lobster example, but a few athletes pulled up with the rims and shoes. Hey, they earned it, and it was up to me to do the same and have those same choices; no hate from me. Some of us walk-ons carried another type of swagger. It usually came from being the hardest workers and just knowing we could get the job done if the opportunity presents; we were just paying our way for the moment.

Some of the scholarship guys were intimidated by us. Especially us that had learned the ropes and knew our roles. There were levels to this, just like in life outside of the college campuses. As the great Jay Z said, "You know the type, loud as a motorbike but wouldn't bust a grape in a fruit fight." I wasn't a locker room guy, someone that talked loudly but didn't deliver on the field.

You have talkers and doers, and not to toot my own horn, but I was the real deal. That's tough for some players to see in their teammates because it scares them. Quiet in the locker room, but loud as a cannon on the field.

You have to have street cred. I earned it, and a few of the vets helped me understand how to translate that ultimate desire to play and perform into game-time. Many of the successes I had on the practice field brought everyone's level of play up around me. Some of the guys weren't feeling the little bit of recognition we got from the coaches. The walk-on crew, Jama Jones, D Mason, and Drian B, had that drive also. They and others showed a lot of love, keeping me encouraged in downtime, telling me how I was one of the team's fastest, hardest-hitting, and best blocking guys on the field. Yeah, that made other players jealous and resentful, but you've only got so many chances to prove yourself, and even with minimal opportunities, I was moving up. At times, I'd noticed how some guys were in their feelings about the changes. Again, I didn't care. I didn't have the time to. I stayed Ray Charles to the bull and kept locked into whatever or whoever I was going to demolish, pushing me toward the next step of the main goal of earning a scholarship.

On the road to success, you've got to take your backpack off every once in a while and sort things out on the ground. Place the things that make you happy and motivate you back in the bag and leave the rest of the crap behind on the floor.

Doing that lightens your load and keeps you from pre-exhaustion before finding a camp for the night. Leaving behind what you don't need helps those watching to grow understanding on what they should dump on their road to success.

There are certain things that you can do to be successful as a walk-on player. As I said, I've dumped most of my petty thoughts to concentrate on the future and what works to move forward efficiently. Now, let me talk to you as what some may consider a successful walk-on to you, future leaders.

Blueprint Island

As I mentioned earlier, you have to be prepared educationally. I slipped-up there. I should have taken my classes more seriously. This could have been pressed if I had gotten with my high school and college counselors and recognized my options. Just keep in mind that your academic counselor probably won't know or care about the NCAA regulations as it pertains to sports. The college will just forward you to the athletics area, and they are always too busy for civilian consultations. Check the rules out for yourself on the internet, and if you're in high school, ask your coaches cause sports rules and regulations change every year.

Physical Preparation. You can't be successful on the field if you aren't physically able. Hit the weights, do your sprints and agility drills. If you're not physically prepared for whatever opportunity presents, then you have wasted your and the person(s) time. Get yourself right or get out the way for the next person.

Mental Preparation. You must know the position you want to play. Ask yourself: Do I know everything about that position? Who is my reference? Do I know the roles of the other positions that are on the field? Do I understand how all the tasks help one another? You're part of a team.

Get noticed, be seen. Before tryouts ever start, visit the facilities. You should ask a department counselor or administrator in the sports complex to see a coach. You won't get to, but you want them to see you. They need to get to know you and understand that you're serious about why you are there. After tryouts start, and even after making the team, be visible. I was kicked off the practice field once or twice by Coach Jackson, but I needed them to know I was serious. He said, "Ay dog, this is a closed practice." But I insistent that I get noticed without being too much of a pest. Once you get in the door, actions speak louder than words, so do something positive that will get the coaches to want to learn your name. One time, I accidentally ran over a guy during a special teams drill, and I heard the head coach ask, "who the fuck is this guy?" That resulted in him putting his two best players on me, getting me a good look on film, and eventually starting on all special teams except field goal and field goal block.

Be versatile. No matter what position you want to play, you've got to be flexible. Be an athlete and a player who learns all aspects of the game so that you can fill in anywhere. Watch all the drills and scrimmages to learn more about the system of your team. I knew that UH's strength was their offense, so I walked-on as a safety but got moved to running back, showing that the coaches saw something in me. The good thing was that I could adjust when I was presented with more opportunities for success. Play anywhere they ask and be reasonable about it. In my senior season, I was asked by a graduate assistant coach to play scout team as I did the two years before. I refused to do because I figured that I had paid my dues and was ready to rep with the starting crew. Even though I had a valid point for how much I had done in the past, I should have remained flexible. This could have possibly caused me to lose the reps that would've earned me the playing time I was seeking. Remember, every day is a tryout for walk-ons.

Know your strengths. If you're a finesse player, that's cool, but don't try to be a banger. Be good enough to accomplish any task you're asked to but stand-out strong in your strengths. If you are shifty, then be shifty, but when the coach asks you to take on that huge linebacker or linemen, buckle that chinstrap and make a play. Be resilient in uncomfortable situations and figure out how to use those strengths to your best advantage.

Know your role. That's a tough one because we all have dreams, but once you're there on the team, walk-ons got to take what's offered. Beggars can't be choosers. Learn what the coaches want from you and be the best you can be at it. You can always aspire for more, but you can't move up if you aren't better at the position you are filling right now! They say, 'you only have to be ten percent better than the next man, but as a walk-on, you have to be ten times better.'

Learn patience. You'll have to wait for an opportunity. Again, when it comes around, you better have your game face on. You are being asked to hit like a Mack Truck when given the opportunity. Since those chances may be few and far between, you will have to have the patience of a saint.

Politics. Yeah, there's a lot of politics in sports. That's because sports are like a business. Sports are businesses with teeth-jarring hits. Sometimes, you've got to go along to get along. Learn what's going on behind the scenes so you can rub shoulders with the right people when you need to. I'm a very private person, but this can leave your teammates or coaches apprehensive about helping you. The right conversation could get you moved from a four to a three giving you more plays, equaling more opportunity to show what you've got.

Compete. That's an everyday job. You don't just make the team and then coast. Scholarship guys are always arriving, not to take your job, because it's theirs already; you've got to take it from them. Every opportunity you get, you have to fight the urge to get complacent. When the hunger fades, so does your game.

I didn't know all these things when I started. It's a learning curve you need to adhere to and follow. The patience thing is real, every day. You get noticed for how you practice, your hitting, and your heart. I wasn't the type of person to make the extra conversation. Just give me the ball and watch me work was how I rolled, but had I sprinkled in a bit more of these philosophies, maybe things could have been slightly different. You have the blueprint, so use it!

Hindsight Island

"Love me or hate me, I stay hate free.
They say we learn from mistakes, well,
that's why they mistake me."

— *Lil Wayne*

I got my degree from the University of Houston in 2013, a Bachelor of Science in Kinesiology.

It was a long time coming from my short downtime after high school - to junior college - and then, the University of Houston. Sometimes, I think I should have stayed in junior college and got another year of play in. Other times, I wish I went with my initial thought and started at a community college and transitioned to the University of North Texas. Then, there was the option to go to Iowa State with my cousin Ter'Ran. Hindsight is 20/20, and everything happens for a reason.

The thing that sticks with me is that it can't be wrong if you have a passion and follow it. My football outcome didn't have much to do with my ability. I played for a particularly good Division 1 team. Getting hurt made a big difference, but sometimes, you're in the right place at the wrong time.

I have the same thinking about our 2012 bowl game. I was emotional about the team having a great season and not being able to play in the bowl, then to add insult to injury, I wrecked my *Explorer* that I had just purchased right before we left for the game. I was a little shook up from the impact but walked away with no major injuries. I look back and see how I was stuck on a mental rollercoaster. I was quick to see myself on a downslope and was so caught up in my main goal that I didn't just sit back and enjoy the ride. There were too many episodes that all I was thinking was what can go wrong will go wrong.

That's a bad way to go through life. When you speak that way, then you tend to lean toward the negative instead of speaking and manifesting positivity into your situation. I certainly don't feel that way now, but I didn't enjoy my football career as I should've. There's a saying that "hard work is its own reward," well, it didn't seem that way to me because I've never shied away from hard work, but I always had a goal I was working towards. I understand now that I have no regrets about how I did my part. The scholarship was the reward to me, but I can only control what I can control.

Along the way, through the muck and mire, I learned to be relentless. I realized it was okay to take two steps forward and one step back as long as I moved towards my goal. I refused to let anyone stop me; they didn't have a chance. Being relentless, that's energy, discipline, and a willingness to be meticulous and coachable. Success is for the gritty people who refuse to give up.

I think I like the saying, "Anything worth having is worth working for," much better. I've worked hard, played hard, and had hard times, but everything I've got now is precious to me; that's as it should be. Nobody should ever be ashamed of what they have or don't have. Sometimes, we just get what we get.

What I got from UH was a bucketful of memories, some good friends, a lot of great coaching tips I use to this day, and an education that can't ever be taken away. Looking back, I wouldn't trade it for anything.

The degree I came away with suits me well. It opened up many opportunities that I'd never have had if I didn't take the leap of faith and try walking on as a football player (at both the JuCo and UH). It also gave me a baseline for what I hope my children will have when they grow up if they want to go to college.

Remember, all my mother's siblings graduated from Mansfield High School. This high school was one of the last desegregated schools in the nation. I'm the first in my immediate family to earn their college degree. With hope, my generation of kids in the family will have many more graduates.

Harvest Island

*"But, hey, I did everything the right way
and earned my spot in this game; nothing
was given to me."*

-Shaquille O'Neal

When I was in high school, I thought I was in the prime of life. Then, when I successfully walked-on at the University of Houston and played football from 2010 through 2012, I once again thought I was in the prime of my life. I was wrong.

My fellow walk-ons and young athletes may wonder why they should take the word of someone who didn't even earn a scholarship or go pro, and I reply in my Kanye voice, "I ain't got all the answers, Sway."

But what I know is that if you look back at my situation and how I handle things, you will see success. Whether it was helping teammates with studying the playbook, route running, proper steps, footwork techniques, or even giving friends and co-workers advice, I do my best to make sure the result is of its highest quality. Even when the situation does not benefit me, I make everyone around me better.

My career ended with zero yards on zero carries with six total offensive plays, never starting as a running back in a recorded game. Was I pissed? You fucking right, but do I have regrets for not doing my part? Negative. When I ask those who were around me, all I hear is how I inspired them as a specialist, a leader and how they hate that I was unable to show the world what I could do as a running back on game day.

Would I have changed anything from my college days? Of course, no one wants to tear their ACL, play football with a dislocated bone in the wrist, live in a car, or have to plan a week's worth of meals with ten dollars to their name. But changing your struggle from the past also affects your character-building process, which in the end helped me to master the system to get in the game.

The knowledge gain pre and post injuries, along with the transitional phases with the coaching staff, gave me the teachings needed to be content with my final chapters in college sports.

Pause Island

At this point, I've given you the game, and now it's time for you to put your period at the end of your sentence. As a matter of fact, why not an exclamation point '!'? Making the team then would make someone consider that a successful walk-on gave me immense satisfaction.

Right now, today, this minute, I'm in the prime of my life! I don't regret the struggles and the adversity I faced because it made me what I am now. I'm a happy, successful man. Of course, adversity still presents itself at times. With the battles of racial injustice on black men every day, I have to second-guess if I should leave the house to remedy a late-night sweet tooth or whether I should take a jog around the block instead of running in circles in my backyard to soothe Jasmine's anxious feelings grown from wrongful deaths due to police brutality. I am blessed that things are good, and there's time to continue to create a great future in front of me.

Some see me as mysterious in ways. They wonder what is going on with him and why is he so quiet? People stare at me in the airports; they tiptoe around and/or squint toward me when we make eye contact as if they are trying to read my mind through telepathy or something. Here's a solution: ask me, "What's on your mind?" but be sure to be prepared for the answer. A lot of the time, it's because I'm in unfamiliar territory or I'm trying to figure out how a problem came about with some solution to the issue that has nothing to do with where I am physically standing at that moment. Even if there is no resolution, I try to have some type of clarification, whatever the matter, a great deal of the time, just for my sanity.

Trying to understand me completely can be a difficult task that even those closest are unable to decipher. So, asking questions will be your best bet.

With all the brain games, "pause," I love my life. "Pause" is a game kids play. When you say something that can be misinterpreted inappropriately, and if you don't say "pause," then your friends act goofy and make fun.

I have a beautiful wife, Jasmine, who's stayed with me through some tough times and brightened my day every step of the way, even after knowing about the ungroomed and stinky kid label. I have an equally beautiful and healthy child that I do my best to make sure that she won't have to go through the hardships that I faced. I'm also blessed with a job that allows me time to mentor children who might just be going through some of the things I faced as a kid.

When I volunteer at camps or feed the homeless, I'm always grateful for what I have, and I always think, "Gee, if I can just help one person today, it's all worth it."

Football was great for me. I developed a work ethic that resonated through every fiber of my being, heart, and soul. I ran into some adversity, and I don't blame the man upstairs for that. He's always got a plan.

Through football, I earned respect from my teammates and my coaches, and I gained respect for myself for seeing adversity as a challenge I could face and eventually overcome. The hard work I continued for the next three years of training, practice, game time, and of course, schoolwork had rewards too. Even after having no college commitment (and no way to pay for college), getting hurt at the junior college, then not being unable to try out for an entire year after transferring to UH paid off for me through my journey in higher education.

I was taught to leave an environment better than it looked when you got there. This analogy generally pertains to cleaning your area at the table as you completed your meal or whatever inside/outside space that we were allowed to play in at my aunt Nanny's house. I chose to carry that thought process into my everyday living. Make every situation better; however, I can, thinking inside and/or outside of the box.

A few ways this became apparent were when Coach Mayberry apologized for cutting me freshmen year, explaining how it was a huge mistake. I received apologies from multiple fellas trying to fight me, which in several ways felt better than winning a fight, and this procedure also led to coaching offers on all levels. I felt that I had lost the battle in those moments, but their words made me feel like the war was won. I had a Graduate Assistant spot offered at UH. After coming home to Mansfield, I got multiple high school coaching offers. I had a middle school coaching offer and even a Pop Warner coaching spot. What I chose was a steady life with my lady and family.

I'm thrilled with the choices I've made, and maybe I wouldn't have chosen them if I hadn't had a mother who decided we needed to move back home. Perhaps, I wouldn't have made the same choices if I hadn't had the church as a huge part of my upbringing. Maybe, the things I'd have done would have been different if I had it easy and didn't face adversity at every turn.

But that would mean I'd have never developed into my true character. I'd have never known where my highs and lows were.

I'd have never met my queen and the love of my life, gone to UH, played collegiate football, and drawn the satisfaction of competing and completing my initial goal, which was to earn a bachelor's degree for my mother and myself.

And, I'd have never had the future I've got in front of me or held the courage of my convictions to say, Yes, I believe in the choices I've made.

Today, I'm a PE Teacher in my hometown, with plenty of friends and family around to keep me busy. I also do lots of community service, like food to the homeless and kids' camps, which are my most important services.

I'm excited for the future, whatever's out there, whatever happens. If I'd had it easy, I wouldn't have the drive to think and try so many things, especially things that are in front of me for myself and my family. How can we miss it?

I also find time to be a Men of Distinction Mentorship Leader, and I'm a volunteer for kid's football camps in my metroplex and places like Hawaii. Every day, I think I'm a lucky man who has it all.

Irreplaceable Island

*"Whatever your life's work is, do it well.
A man should do his job so well that the
living, the dead, and the unborn could do
it no better."*

-Martin Luther King, Jr.

My story isn't just about football, though it seems like it is since I've been yappin' about it most of this text. The truth is, football is just a metaphor in my life. Adversity and how we can all overcome it is my real story.

Everyone is going to encounter adversity and hardship in their life. It's inevitable, a part of life that gives us tasks that our mind and spirit desperately need though difficult. The pride and fulfillment you get from a job well done, especially when difficult, uplift and nourish the soul. But you already knew that.

Of course, the problem is finding a way to overcome what we often perceive as 'insurmountable odds,' adversity that looms in the distance and seems at times too much even to consider facing. Sometimes, it seems that even admitting that we have hardship and adversity in our lives is tough. I didn't know things were tough when I was little because I had no reference. When I grew up and found out that things could be better and should be better, I slowly acknowledged those bumps in my life might be real roadblocks that had to be dealt with to succeed.

In many ways, my church gave me an excellent foundation for life. Had I not been at multiple services during the week, I'm sure there would have been more misfortune waiting for me. I didn't learn everything at church, but I did learn a lot. And I remember much of what they taught me.

Proverbs 24:10 says: "If you faint in the day of adversity, your strength is small."

That might not give you much inspiration, but I know it comes back to me regularly. Today, I see adversity as a challenge, and I never let my resolve or strength be small, as the proverb says.

Proverbs 17:17 says: A friend loves at all times, and a brother is born for adversity.

To me, that means it's alright to lean on a friend or your family for help. They are there for you when you need them if you have the simple courtesy to ask. Most people don't consider it a burden when asked for help; they are flattered. If you can't see a way out, ask for help.

If you are going at it alone, well, God bless you; have faith in yourself and the Lord. He is with you every step of the way. Still, life is easier with a helping hand from a friend or loved one. I've gotten that sturdy hold from my family numerous times, and my wife has a grip that won't ever let me fall.

I also like a few simple words from Drake, who said, "Life can always change; you just have to adjust."

"Well, ain't that the truth," in my Aunt Esther's voice! A true constant in life is that things can and will change. It has to; nature won't allow stagnation. For people, change usually happens just when you think things are finally going right. A lot of us react to the extremes of the really bad or great, losing sight of all the small but incredible good things. When you fall into the pessimistic thought that things can't get any worse, you have to flip that mindset; either way, it's coming. Since you know it's coming; there's no reason you can't be prepared for it!

When I was a kid, aside from being hungry, I didn't think things were too bad. We might not have had what our friends had, but it was what it was. So, I found something to amuse myself. I listened to my folks and handled things the best I could. If I've learned anything in this life, it's how you face adversity that makes the difference. I don't run from it. I now stand up to it like a rock.

Marathon Island

*"I have discovered in life that there are
ways of getting almost anywhere you
want to go if you really want to go."*
— *Langston Hughes*

After all these years, my folks seem to have worked things out and are doing well. There's nothing like taking your kids to see grandma and grandpa and seeing a healthy and happy family together. My mother now works as a director at one of the schools as the cafeteria coordinator, so she's busy, never too busy for us, though. My brother and sister are doing okay. I get to visit them regularly.

I'm optimistic about the future. I learned that as a child, no matter what came along, when you fail, you've got to get back up and see yourself getting better. Having that mindset, that idea, that blueprint for life, can change the world, one small step at a time.

So, whatever's out there, whatever happens, be prepared and flexible. Accept hardship easily and commit to taking on the challenges that life presents, no matter how difficult. If I'd had it easy, I wouldn't have the drive to think and try so many things. Don't be upset with the hurdles; with the Walk-On Island mentality, how can we miss?

Have a plan for where you want to go. I couldn't have gotten here or had a chance to move forward if it wasn't for my drive and the many people in my life. I'd have never been on the path I'm on if I hadn't been honest with myself and admitted when I was wrong. I had to grow up fast and learn that the smartest thing is never to stop learning. I now understand that there was more to my upbringing, similar to my dad's, but not holding a candle in his struggle of being a drug kingpin's son. It gave me the courage to go forward. I trust myself.

As the saying goes, I went the extra mile. What I found is that the extra mile is a vast, unpopulated place of beauty. Nonbelievers haven't spoiled it; just the opposite.

People say they go the extra mile, but most of them talk and don't make it because it's a land filled with booby traps and roadblocks, but enough of that. Just know that the extra mile is worth the journey because the place you reach is filled with opportunities.

I had the lucky opportunity for many things, including some great friends who have stuck with me over the years, like Greg, David, Darius, John, James, and Randy, another guy I met in school. We're cool, and I talk to most of them at least twice a month.

I enjoy being a father and a husband, but there's more now. Right here, I'm enjoying being an author, a motivational speaker, and maybe, just maybe, there's a future for me as a professional musician.

Today's adversity and the roadblocks I see are minor bumps in the road. I just have to be honest about them, make a plan to beat them, and take the next step. You can do the same if you want, and I wish you great success in the process!

I hope the adversity you face doesn't include losing a leg, but no matter what roadblocks are out there for us, there's always a path forward.

In many areas of life, people will quit. They'll look at their situation, the long odds against success, and they'll take the easy way out and quit. Let them choose their fate. Know that you've got the strength to hang on, no matter what the world throws your way.

CPSIA information can be obtained
at www.ICGtesting.com
Printed in the USA
BVHW051731210523
664592BV00006B/73

9 781735 973937